Sex, Priestly Ministry, and the Church

Len Sperry, M.D., Ph.D.

Foreword by
Donald Cozzens

LITURGICAL PRESS
Collegeville, Minnesota

www.litpress.org

Dedication

This book is dedicated to fond memory of the late James J. Gill, S.J., M.D., who was both a friend and mentor to me and an inspiration and the epitome of priestly ministry to many.

Acknowledgments

My heartfelt appreciation to Linda Amadeo for her friendship and sage advice over many years, to Donald Cozzens for taking time out of a very busy schedule to review and write the book's foreword, and to the staff at the Liturgical Press who made this project a reality: Linda Maloney, Mark Twomey, Aaron Raverty, O.S.B., Colleen Stiller, and Peter Dwyer.

Cover design by Greg Becker

2	3	4	5	6	7	8

Library of Congress Cataloging-in-Publication Data

Sperry, Len.
    Sex, priestly ministry, and the Church / Len Sperry.
        p. cm.
    "A Michael Glazier book."
    Includes bibliographical references and index.
    ISBN 0-8146-2967-9 (alk. paper)
    1. Child sexual abuse by clergy.   2. Catholic Church—Clergy—Sexual behavior. 3. Catholic Church—Discipline. I. Title.

BX1912.9.S67 2003
261.8'3272'08822—dc21   2003047611

Contents

Foreword

It is not an exaggeration to claim that the clergy sexual abuse scandal of the past three decades has shaken the very foundations of the Catholic Church. And the tremors promise to be felt for years to come. Wave upon wave of Catholics have come forward with tragic reports of being sexually abused by priests and bishops while in their childhood or adolescence. And in a sad, almost pathetic attempt to avoid scandal, Church officials have themselves provoked a scandal of unprecedented magnitude by their pastoral and administrative bungling that in many cases wounded again the victims who should have been their primary concern. As a result, American bishops—with their credibility in tatters—find themselves facing an angry, disillusioned Catholic laity. A cardinal archbishop has resigned, a half a dozen or so bishops have been pressured out of office, and more than a thousand U.S. priests have had formal allegations of sexual abuse or misconduct brought against them.

While Church leaders have made serious and significant strides in bringing a halt to the abuse and putting in place policies and norms to block priest perpetrators from abusing again, the impression is given that once review boards are in place, the policies strictly implemented, and the lawsuits settled, we can get back to the way things were prior to the scandal. Little if any discussion is heard from Church authorities about the *meaning* of the abuse scandal, about the *institutional factors* unwittingly contributing to the crisis, about the *etiology* of the current, tragic nightmare. Catholics and the general population are led to believe the scandal is about human weakness, pure and simple—a few bad apples in an otherwise healthy barrel. This "spin," however, is not taking hold. Sooner or later, if U.S. bishops are to recover their moral authority, an honest, in-depth, and candid analysis must be made of the clergy abuse scandal. Such an analysis will likely reveal the need for systemic and structural changes in the Catholic Church—and, therefore, will be resisted by Catholics who view the present clerical structure itself as divinely ordained. In spite of the anticipated resistance, nothing is more urgently needed than a thorough inquiry into meaning, institutional factors, and the etiology of the abuse scandal.

Those conducting such an inquiry, as well as all who want to understand this tragic chapter in American Catholicism, have at their disposal an exceptional tool in Len Sperry's latest book *Sex, Priestly Ministry, and the Church*. There is nothing quite like it! It is at the same time foundational and developmental, clinical and clear, scientific and pastoral, comprehensive and concise. Case studies are deftly presented and the author's clarity of expression combine to make this a remarkably readable book. Sperry's significant accomplishment will not only prove an essential resource for our understanding of the factors that have contributed to the present crisis, but also for our efforts in building a renewed and healthier ministerial presence in the Church.

Without question, this well organized and well-researched volume deserves a wide reading—from bishops to priests, from the Keating Commission to diocesan review boards, from pastoral educators to parents, from journalists to the general public.

Rev. Donald Cozzens, Ph.D.,
author of *The Changing Face of
the Priesthood* and *Sacred Silence*

Introduction

"Would removing the celibacy requirement really eliminate priest pedophilia?" "Aren't they really talking about gender identity development rather than psychosexual development?" "Isn't it ephebophilia when the minor is more than thirteen years old?" "Won't implementing the provisions of bishops' charter only exacerbate the priest shortage?" These types of questions reflect the kinds of concerns many of us are thinking and talking about lately. Despite all the media attention, articles, and studies on sexual impropriety in the Church, there is relatively little known about sexuality issues involving priests. While it is true that some terms like psychosexual development are elusive and beg for definitional clarity, and some issues are ideological fodder—for example, that celibacy is the root cause of pedophilia—the fact is that there is a dearth of understanding and intelligibility in too many discussions of these matters. While ignorance and imprecise thinking may be excused among outsiders, there is little excuse when those within Church circles are without the necessary information and guidelines needed to make informed decisions on key issues such as removing accused priests from active ministry. Unfortunately, when these leaders and formation personnel are without sufficient information and guidelines, their decisions tend to be made on the basis of opinion or ideology.

At a time when pundits are making radical proposals like scrapping the seminary system, and when the lives of well-regarded priests with a single, distant allegation of sexual impropriety are in turmoil because of the threat of being removed from active ministry, the stakes are much too high to base such weighty decisions on limited knowledge and criteria. Unfortunately, many in need-to-know situations have either little or no access to such objective sources, or they must wade through the available but ideologically biased books and articles to find snippets of usable information. Currently there is no single resource to turn to for an objective and complete description of the essential terms and key background information on sexual issues facing the Church. Neither is there a single source that clarifies issues and provides useful guidelines to inform decision-making at both the policy level and the implementation and formation levels. A source that provides both information and guidelines—in an objective and non-ideological fashion—would be invaluable and is sorely needed. *Sex, Priestly Ministry, and the Church* attempts to fill that need.

In many ways, this book is a one-of-a-kind resource. It is a concise, comprehensive, authoritative, and up-to-date source for the kind of information needed to understand current controversies and make reasoned, responsible decisions. It is divided into three sections or parts. Part I begins by providing the reader with a working vocabulary of the fifty-plus essential terms and ideas at the heart of current concerns and issues. Next, it walks the reader through the entire process of psychosexual development and the various factors—hormonal, psychological, and family and social—that impact development. An integrative *model of psychosexual development* is described and illustrated in order to clarify and increase the reader's understanding of both the normal and pathological outcomes of the biological, psychological, social, and religious and spiritual processes involved in sexual development. This integrative model provides a diagnostic map for assessing ministry candidates for formation and ordination.

While Part I focuses primarily on healthy sexual development, Part II describes the causes of priest sexual misconduct involving children, adolescents, and adults. It begins with a discussion of four determinants of sexual misconduct: the priest's personality and psychosexual development; the structure and culture of his religious organization; the stressors and supportiveness of his current ministry assignment; and his relationships with vulnerable parishioners. The influences of abusiveness and narcissistic entitlement on the priest's professional identity are then described. Following a brief discussion of the question whether pedophilia and ephebophilia are criminal offenses, immoral actions, or psychiatric disorders, a *vulnerability model of priest sexual misconduct* is described and illustrated. The clinical value and administrative utilization of this vulnerability model are further discussed in Part III.

Part III describes a number of pressing issues, including some that are quite controversial, facing the Church today. These include choosing suitable candidates for priestly ministry, removing priests from the active ministry, preventing sexual misconduct, and the debate on homosexuality. Beyond simply describing these issues, the book provides guidelines and methods for dealing with these issues.

This book has been developed around a few research-based premises. Two of these premises bear mentioning here. The first is that psychosexual development occurs within the context of human development and includes biological, psychological, social, and religious and spiritual dimensions or lines of development. The social dimension is broad and includes the immense, albeit subtle, impact of the structure and culture of religious institutions on a priest's sexual attitudes and behaviors. A second premise is that psychosexual development in priests is an ongoing process for which the ultimate goal is the integration of sexuality and intimacy. Since the priesthood requires celibacy, this sexuality-intimacy integration must necessarily include celibacy. Accordingly, priests with high levels of psychosexual development tend to be effective in ministry because they are psychologically and spiritually mature.

In short, this book is about psychosexual development from birth through adulthood, how this developmental process is influenced by various biological, psychological, social, and religious and spiritual factors, and how this developmental process impacts a priest's personal and professional functioning. The reader is taken on a guided tour of this developmental process and the various healthy and unhealthy trajectories or paths this process takes, including sexual misconduct with children, adolescents, and adults. It is also a book about the critical and pressing issues and controversies surrounding the sexuality of ministers and priests.

Sex, Priestly Ministry, and the Church should be of interest to a broad spectrum of individuals concerned about the sexual issues facing the Church today. Some will be in leadership positions in dioceses and religious orders who are responsible for making decisions regarding various sexual issues. Some will be members of diocesan lay review boards charged with reviewing cases and making recommendations about retaining or removing priests from ministry. Some will be faculty and formation personnel in seminaries, theologates, and ministry-training programs who teach courses, advise, or provide spiritual direction to seminarians and other ministry personnel. Some will be students taking university or seminary courses and seminars on sexuality. Others will be priests and ministry personnel in parishes and other ministry settings. Still others will be lay individuals concerned about the future of the priesthood and the Church.

Even though the current situation involving priests and the Church may seem somewhat bleak, I feel hopeful that out of the wake of this crisis a new and revitalized priestly ministry and model of Church will emerge. It is my sincere hope that this book will serve, in some small way, to foster that change by promoting healthy psychosexual development in priests and other ministry personnel.

Chapter 1

Sex and Sexuality: Everything You Need to Know

Pedophilia, ephebophilia, gender identity, psychosexual development, paraphilias! While these terms are commonplace in print and television reports, unfortunately, there seems to be relatively little understanding of the meaning of these and other terms. It is indeed ironic that for years sexuality was scarcely discussed openly in Christian circles and now there seems to be few other topics that are more widely discussed or are more urgent. Regrettably, many of these discussions seem uninformed or at least less focused than they might otherwise be since there is yet to be a shared understanding of these terms and concepts. While this chapter does not portend to be the definitive compendium of terminology on sex and sexuality, it does attempt to offer a reasonably objective description and definitions of several concepts necessary for understanding the current issues without any ideological axes to grind or positions to support.

Some fifty commonly used terms and concepts are briefly defined and described or illustrated. These terms have been catalogued in five main categories: sex and sexuality, sexual and gender development, intimacy and sexuality, sexual and gender orientations, and sexual difficulties and disorders. Rather than being listed in alphabetical order, as in a glossary, the terms are logically sequenced wherein basic concepts are first described and defined and subsequent terms build on these concepts. Table 1-1 lists these terms.

1

Table 1-1: Sexuality Terms

Sex and Sexuality
Sex
Sexuality
Sexual Practices
Orgasm
Sexual Health
Sexually Healthy Family
Sexual and Gender Development
Psychosexual
Psychosexual Development
Psychosexual Maturity [i.e., Integrated Sexuality]
Sexual Orientation
Sexual Identity
Gender Identity
Gender-Role Stereotyping
Intimacy and Sexuality
Intimacy
Pseudo-Intimacy
Sexual and Nonsexual Intimacy
Celibate Intimacy
Celibate Sexuality
Barriers to Intimacy
Sexuality and Spirituality
Sexual and Gender Orientations
Androgyny
Heterosexuality
Homosexuality
Homophobia
Rating Scale for Sexual Orientation
Situational Homosexuality
Lesbianism
Bisexuality
Transgenderism
Transexualism

Sexual Difficulties and Disorders
Fixation
Boundaries
Sexual Offender
Sexual Abuse
Vulnerability
Sexual Misconduct
Sexual Harassment
Abusiveness and the Abusive Personality
Sexual Addiction
Sexual Compulsivity
Paraphilias
Pedophilia
Pedophile
Fixated Pedophile
Regressed Pedophile
Ephebophilia
Ephebophile
Fixated Ephebophile
Regressed Ephebophile
NMBLA
Impairment
Professional Distress
Unfitness for Ministry

Sex and Sexuality

Sex: The term sex has two common designations. The first refers to the biological aspect of one's personhood, the individual's biological makeup based on the appearance of genitals—male or female, i.e., who we are. The second refers to genital behavior, i.e., what we think, feel and do sexually. This includes arousal and activities associated with sexual feelings, fantasies, masturbation, foreplay or intercourse for the purpose of pleasure and/or reproduction.

Sexuality: Sexuality encompasses both sex, i.e., who we are and what we think, feel and do sexually, as well as the meanings given to sex. "What our body means to us, how we understand ourself as a woman or as a man, the way we feel comfortable in expressing affection— these are part of our sexuality. . . . In this broadest sense, sexuality is how we make sex significant" (Whitehead and Whitehead 1989:45). While sexuality typically involves some such physical indications or caring and concern such as touching, it does not necessarily include genital intercourse or related sexual practices.

Sexual Practices: Refers to a variety of *sexual activity* including penile-vaginal sex, foreplay, masturbation, anal sex, or oral sex which may or may not lead to orgasm.

Orgasm: Orgasm is the brief, intense sensations in the genitals—which can spread throughout the body—experienced during the peak or climax of sexual arousal and response. It is characterized by a series of highly pleasurable contractions of pelvic muscles accompanying the discharge of sexual tension. It can also include ejaculation in males.

Sexual Health: Sexual health refers to attitudes, behaviors and relationships about sexuality. It also refers to the absence of sexually transmitted diseases. *Sexually healthy persons* are individuals who view sexuality in positive terms, are comfortable with their own sexuality, and can relate to others in a sexually and emotionally responsible manner while maintaining appropriate boundaries.

Sexually Healthy Family: Sexually healthy persons typically develop within sexually healthy families. These are families where both personal identities and the integrity of the family system are maintained and boundaries are respected between the sexes. Such families hold developmentally appropriate values for sexuality and family members experience positive forms of touch and physical interaction without emotional or physical invasiveness (Friberg and Laaser 1998).

Sexual and Gender Development

Psychosexual: Psychosexual refers to the emotional and/or cognitive aspects of sexuality.

Psychosexual Development: Psychosexual development—referred to increasingly today as gender identity development—is a commonly used but elusive term for which there is little consensus on its exact meaning and method of assessment. While the psychoanalytic perspective has been much criticized it is nevertheless widely known. In this perspective, psychosexual development is a stage-by-stage process of growth of sexuality as it affects personality development. Freud believed that the need for erotic gratification is present from birth onward and its driving force or energy, libido, is a basic motivation for growth. This process of development typically proceeds through five stages each associated with a specific erogenous zone where libido is focused: oral, anal, phallic, latency, and genital. Such development is normal or uneventful for many individuals, while stunted or "fixated" for others. For Freud, "normal" psychosexual development meant internalizing cultural norms, identifying with the same-sex parent, and achieving sexual gratification with members of the opposite sex. When fixated, an adult continues to seek gratification in ways that are appropriate only to children or adolescents (Freud 1924/1968:322–37; Craig and Baucom 2002:44–45).

It should be noted that there are two other lesser known theories of psychosexual or gender identity development, which are Social Learning Theory and Cognitive-Developmental Theory (Longres 2000). Nevertheless, in the absence of an empirically validated theory of sexual development, most people, including many religious leaders and formation personnel, essentially subscribe to Freud's psychosexual development theory even though they believe that psychosocial and psychosexual growth is also influenced by other factors, including spiritual and religious values. It has been said that the goal of psychosexual development is not orgasm but rather the mature capacity to love (Goergen 1974:180). A high level of psychosexual development is called psychosexual maturity.

Psychosexual Maturity: Psychosexual maturity refers to the highest level of psychosexual development wherein an individual has successfully completed the psychosexual developmental tasks associated with adolescents and adulthood (DeLamater and Friedrich 2002:12). In the monumental National Conference of Catholic Bishops' sponsored study of Catholic priests in the United States, four levels of psychological development among priests were reported. These four levels represented a continuum of development from lowest to highest: (1) maldeveloped, (2) underdeveloped, (3) developing, and (4) developed. Researchers found that psychosexual development (which they called "psychosexual maturity") was the best predictor or the "developed" level, while psychosocial development (based on Erikson's stage mode of development) was the second best predictor (Kennedy and Heckler 1971:171).

Sexual Orientation: Sexual orientation refers to the emotional and erotic preference for the category of people—heterosexual, homosexual, or bisexual—an individual *prefers* to relate to sexually or intimately.

The operative word here is "preference" amid clear alternatives. For instance, when access to preferred sexual partners is denied or limited, otherwise heterosexual male prison inmates may engage in homosexual activity. This is called *situational homosexuality*. An alternative view of sexual orentation is based on arousal rather than preference (Storms 1981).

Sexual Identity: Sexual identity refers to the individual's *self-identification* as heterosexual, gay, lesbian, or bisexual. "Self-identification" is the operative word which is indicative of whether the individual considers himself or herself as male or female. Sexual identity also refers to whether the individual considers himself or herself to be attractive to others. Sexual identify is related to but different from *gender identity*.

Gender Identity: Gender identity refers to the individual's *subjective sense* of being a man or woman. This sense is typically acquired by the age of three. While *sex* is a biological designation, *gender* is a socially constructed designation. Closely related to gender identity is *gender role,* which is the set of socially and culturally specific norms of attitudes and behaviors expected of men and women. Furthermore, *gender role identity* is the extent to which the individual actually internalizes those expected attitudes and behaviors. In other words, gender identity is the individual's inner sense of self as a man or woman, while gender role is the outward expression of what the individual feels, thinks, says and does that demonstrates to others that he or she is a man or a woman. Moreover, gender role and identity are reflected in masculinity and femininity. Finally, *sexual identity* can appear to differ from gender identity. For example, an individual with a decided heterosexual preference and identification who displays some feminine traits and relatively few classic masculine characteristics could be considered by others to have a homosexual orientation.

Gender-Role Stereotyping: Gender-role stereotyping refers to oversimplified, rigid, preconceived beliefs about the gender roles of men and women. These beliefs can encompass behavioral, psychological, emotional, or religious characteristics. Gender stereotyping can take two forms. In the first, an individual may exhibit a number of characteristics associated with one gender and claim not to have or value the characteristics of the other gender. For instance, a priest may boast a macho image and verbally or nonverbally disparage other males who exhibit more feminine or refined tastes. In the second instance, an individual would be considered gender stereotyped if others make negative attributions about that individual because he exhibited some or many characteristics associated with the opposite gender. For example, parishioners may comment to others about a priest's effeminate mannerisms and question his sexual orientation.

Intimacy and Sexuality

Intimacy: Intimacy refers to those feelings in a relationship that promote closeness or bondedness *and* the experience of warmth. This sense of closeness can include emotional, intellectual, social, and spiritual bonds. However, not all close relationships are intimate. For example, while you may work closely with a colleague, the relationship would not be considered intimate unless the second component, i.e., the experience of warmth and affection, is present. Intimacy is a close, familiar and often affectionate personal relationship with another person which involves an in-depth knowledge of the person as well as a proactive expression of one's thoughts, feelings and sentiments which serve as a token of familiarity (Bagarozzi 1999:66). Such closeness in friendships or in romantic relationships often entails ambivalent feelings, both positive and negative, which coexist. "Maturity in intimacy means learning to live with both the exhilaration and the strain that comes with being close" (Whitehead and Whitehead 1989:5). Genital expression may or may not play a role in intimate relationships, just as intimacy may or may not accompany sexual activity.

Pseudo-Intimacy. Pseudo-intimacy reflects a relationship which appears to involve intimacy but, in actuality, does not. In pseudo-intimacy intense sexual feelings typically substitute for genuine intimacy, and the true nature of a relationship is kept secret in order to maintain a fiction that a caring relationship exists and to avoid confrontation.

Sexual and Nonsexual Intimacy: Sexual intimacy refers to the sexuality in an intimate relationship in all its variations ranging from gentle touch to genital intercourse. It is eroticized intimacy and thus can be distinguished from non-eroticized or nonsexual intimacy. **Nonsexual intimacy** includes *emotional intimacy* and *social intimacy,* i.e., a sense of closeness with another person without genital expression. It can include *intellectual intimacy,* which involves "the sharing of ideas and ideals, speaking from both mind and heart while grappling with questions of importance to the world and to one's particular life" (Kenel 2002:30). Finally, it can also include *spiritual intimacy,* i.e., a sense of closeness with God.

Celibate Intimacy. Celibate intimacy is the capacity to share a deep friendship without being married and without violating chastity physically or psychologically. For a priest this form of intimacy is considered by some to be a gift and a grace (Cozzens 2000).

Celibate Sexuality: Similar to the notion of celibate intimacy, celibate sexuality is an expression of sexuality that is centered on friendship and which strives after nongenital intimacy (Goergen 1974).

Barriers to Intimacy: Barriers to intimacy refer to specific behaviors, skill deficits or dispositions which effectively block or protect an individual from forming or maintaining a close bond with another. These include fear of engulfment, lack of trust, limited capacity for empathy, insensitive communication, self-deception, perfectionism, isolation, and failure to achieve a sense of personal identity. In and of itself, the presence of a character disorder or personality disorder, such as the narcissistic, borderline, or antisocial personality disorder, is a major barrier to intimacy.

Sexuality and Spirituality: Sexuality can be viewed in relationship to spirituality. Among the many ways of describing spirituality is a patterning of life around the experience of God (Nelson 1988:24). If it can be assumed "that being created in the image of God to seek and enjoy close communion is a basic human quality and that our psychological development from infancy is built around that characteristic, we identify a helpful theological principle. This points toward the reality that our spiritual life is bound to our psychological development" (Friberg and Laaser 1998:33). Since psychological development inevitably includes sexual development, spirituality and sexuality are integrally related. Finally, spirituality can also be related to intimacy, such that spiritual intimacy is described as a sense of closeness and bonding with God.

Sexual and Gender Orientations

Androgyny: The ability of an individual to display a variety of masculine and feminine traits or behaviors depending on which is appropriate in a given situation. Androgyny implies that an individual can be both compassionate and assertive, emotional and logical, as well as determined and free-spirited, depending on the circumstances.

Heterosexuality: Heterosexuality is sexual desire or behavior directed toward an individual or individuals of the opposite sex. In Western cultures heterosexuals are sometimes referred to as *"straight."*

Homosexuality: Homosexuality is sexual desire or behavior directed toward an individual or individuals of one's same sex. In Western cultures male homosexuals are sometimes referred to as *"gay"* although in some places it is used to refer to homosexuals of either sex. ***Homophobia*** is an irrational fear of homosexuality or homosexual individuals.

Rating Scale for Sexual Orientation: In the 1940s a group of sex researchers headed by Alfred Kinsey developed a 7-point rating scale called the "Rating Scale for Sexual Orientation" to describe and measure sexual orientation. On this scale 0 represents individuals with an *exclusively heterosexual orientation* while 6 represents individuals with an *exclusively homosexual orientation*. Individuals with ratings of 1 or 5 were considered to have *predominantly heterosexual* (1), or *predominantly homosexual* (5) orientations, while individuals with ratings of 2, 3, or 4 were regarded as having bisexual orientations.

Recent scientifically conducted surveys indicate that about 3–5 percent of adult American males and about 1 percent of adult American females are homosexual. These data—and that of similar studies—do not support the commonly held belief among many that at least 10 percent of the adult population in America is gay or lesbian (King 2002).

Situational Homosexuality: Situational homosexuality refers to heterosexuals who engage in homosexual behavior when their access to heterosexual behavior is limited or denied, such as in prisons, boarding schools, etc. (Sperry 2000a).

Lesbianism: Lesbianism refers to the sexual orientation in which a female has a preference for, attraction to, and/or engages in sexual behavior with a woman or women. ***Lesbians*** are female homosexuals.

Bisexuality: Bisexuality refers to the sexual orientation in which an individual has a preference for, attraction to, and/or engages in sexual behavior with both women and men. Relatively little is know about bisexuality in terms of numbers and percentage of the population or how their relationships differ from exclusively heterosexual or homosexual individuals. Furthermore, there is little consensus among researchers on what constitutes bisexuality, including whether it is an enduring trait rather than simply a matter of convenience or expedience.

Transgenderism: Transgenderism refers to the continuum along which individuals engage in *behaviors* that are associated with the other gender. ***Transgender*** refers to an individual whose gender roles and behaviors, such as cross-dressing, are opposite of those that the culture expects based on his or her anatomy.

Transsexualism: Transsexualism refers to the intense, prolonged psychological distress with one's biological sex, often leading the individual to seek surgery to "correct" the condition. A *transsexual* is an adult whose gender identity does not match his or her biological sex.

Sexual Difficulties and Disorders

Fixation: a development "arrest" or failure to achieve a developmental task at an earlier stage of psychosexual development which causes the adult to act in a less than age-appropriate fashion in given situations or to seek gratification in ways that are only appropriate for children or adolescents.

Boundaries: Boundaries are norms, rules, or codes of conduct that characterize an individual's personal space or environment and his or her sense of security and safety. Healthy boundaries provide a nurturing and safe physical, emotional, sexual, and spiritual environment for individuals. Unhealthy boundaries do not provide this type of environment because they are too rigid, loose or inconsistent and are intentionally or inadvertently violated by others. The statements "you're standing too close" or "she's invading my personal space" reflect boundary violations.

Boundary issues for priests are complex and may create boundary challenges and strain that differs from other helping professionals such as physicians or psychotherapists. For example, in addition to presiding at liturgical services, a priest may provide pastoral counseling and spiritual direction, or engage in activities such as leading committee meetings, raising funds, and attending social activities, all with the same parishioners. This multiplicity of roles would likely be unethical for a psychotherapist based on the principle of *dual relationships* (Gonsiorek 1999). Besides being the source of considerable stress and strain, such boundary challenges are important considerations in determining if and how a priest should remain, be removed from, or returned to active ministry.

Sexual Offender: A sexual offender is defined as an adult (a) who has sexual contact with a minor for the purpose of becoming sexually aroused, or (b) who has sexual contact with age-appropriate adults wherein the sexual advance is unwanted or out of control (Bryant 1999:89). Three forms of *clergy sexual offenders* can be described: (1) *pedophilia* wherein sexual preoccupation and behavior is with prepubescent children; (2) *ephebophilia* wherein sexual preoccupation and behavior is with postpubescent minor adolescents; and (3) **adult sexual abuse** or **adult sexual misconduct** wherein sexual preoccupation and behavior are with age-appropriate males or females and sexual advances are unwanted, compulsive, out of control, and/or involve boundary violations. Such behaviors include: sexual harassment, sexual intercourse, fondling, physical force, fellatio or cunnilingus, or rape.

Best estimates "suggest that approximately 6 percent of Catholic priests have been sexually involved with minors with the vast majority of these offenders (about 80 percent or more) targeting postpubescent boys. . . . The number of clergy sexually involved with consenting adults is unknown" (Plante 1999:172).

Sexual Abuse: Sexual abuse is the invasion of an individual's sexual *boundaries* by someone who possesses emotional, physical, or spiritual influence or power over the individual. Sexual abuse inevitably damages psychologically vulnerable individuals.

Vulnerability: Vulnerability is a condition in which there is a reduced capacity to face and resist invasion of one's boundaries.

Sexual Misconduct: Sexual misconduct refers to a breach of professional relationship and involves any sexual action considered immoral or illegal. Sexual misconduct involves such sexual actions committed by a professional that violate an individual's boundaries. Thus, due to their status as professional ministers, sexual abuse perpetrated by priests on parishioners or others within the purview of the priest's ministry is more accurately called sexual misconduct.

Sexual Harassment: Sexual harassment is the use of emotional, financial, social, or organizational power or influence to gain sexual access to or dominance over a person who is vulnerable to that influence. It can involve, whether it be intended or not, the creation of a hostile environment in which words, actions, artwork, or humor causes such discomfort for individuals that they cannot function effectively within that environment (Friberg and Laaser:xi).

Abusiveness and the Abusive Personality: Abusiveness refers to the characteristic pattern of abusive behavior—physical, verbal, emotional, and/or sexual abuse—that characterizes the abusive personality. Individuals with an abusive personality do not necessarily act abusively at all times and in all situations but rather in specific situations and circumstances that activate the pattern of abusiveness. Common to all forms of abuse is emotional abuse. Research indicates that emotional abuse can serve as a proxy for physical and sexual abuse.

For instance, an emotionally abusive gesture or comment may remind a sexually abused individual that he or she can be sexually abused or beaten at any time. Underlying the abusive pattern is the theme of dominance or power of subjugation. The abusive personality is preoccupied with control, controlling how others think, feel and act (Sperry 2000a). Many fixated pedophiles and ephebophiles display the abusive personality.

Sexual Addiction: Sexual addiction refers to a pathological relationship to any form of sexual activity that has become unmanageable and which progressively worsens and usually results in negative consequences (Carnes 1983; 1991).

Sexual Compulsivity: Sexual compulsivity refers to the loss of ability to choose freely whether to stop or continue a sexual behavior. It also refers to situations where there is continuation of the behavior despite adverse consequences and the compulsive continues despite efforts to cease or reduce the frequency of these behaviors. Compulsive behaviors are furthered exacerbated and reinforced by accompanying obsessions, i.e., obsessive thoughts (Bryant 1999).

Paraphilias: A paraphilia is a class of psychosexual disorders in which a deviant form or intensity of sexual behavior is needed to experience sexual excitement, arousal, and gratification. DSM-IV recognizes and describes eight types of paraphilias. These include *exhibitionism,* e.g., exposing one's genitals to unsuspecting strangers; *fetishism,* e.g., holding an inanimate object such as women's panties while masturbating; *frotteurism,* e.g., touching or rubbing against a nonconsensual person; *sexual masochism,* e.g., making another to suffer by humiliation, beating or bondage; *sexual sadism,* e.g., inflicting suffering on a victim; *transvestic fetishism,* e.g., intense arousal involving cross-dressing; *voyeurism,* e.g., observing an unsuspecting person disrobe or engage in sex; and *pedophilia* as described in the next section.

Pedophilia: Pedophilia refers to the sexual activity by adults with a prepubescent child, age thirteen or younger. Such activity can involve undressing the child, exposing one's genitals, masturbating in the presence of the child, touching and fondling, or performing fellatio or cunnilingus, or penetrating the child with a penis, finger, or other objects. Currently, pedophilia is considered a grave moral failing, a legal offense, *and* a sexual psychiatric disorder, called a psychosexual disorder or paraphilia in DSM-IV-TR (American Psychiatric Association 2000). Legally, most state laws designate sexual behavior between an adult and a child under the age of twelve or thirteen to constitute pedophilia, which is a felony, irrespective of the number of times a child is sexually assaulted. DSM-IV-TR specifies three criteria that must be met in order for the diagnosis of pedophilia to be given. First, the adult must experience, over a period of at least six months, recurrent, intense sexually arousing fantasies, sexual urges, or behaviors involving sexual activity with a prepubescent minor. Second, the individual must have acted on these sexual urges, or the sexual urges or fantasies that cause the individual marked distress or interpersonal difficulty. Third, the individual must be at least sixteen years old and be at least five years older than the child or children (American Psychiatric Association 2000).

A *pedophile* is an adult who is sexually attracted to prepubescent children. Different types of pedophiles can be described. DSM-IV-TR distinguishes pedophiles as "exclusive types," i.e., those attracted only to children, and "nonexclusive" types who while primarily attracted to children are sometimes attracted to adults. A more commonly observed distinction is between fixated and regressed pedophilia (Groth, Hobson, and Gary 1982). A *fixated pedophile* is described as an individual whose primary sexual interest is in children and rarely, if ever, engages in sex with peers. These individuals typically are involved with child pornography, may masturbate compulsively, or often use alcohol or other drugs for their disinhibiting effect. They tend to be calculating rather than impulsive in their sexual exploits and use cunning, deceit, and intimidation. There is growing consensus that these individuals are psychosexually immature and developmentally fixated. On the other hand, a *regressed pedophile* is described as an individual whose primary sexual orientation is toward adults of the opposite sex. When under extreme stress such individuals can psychologically regress to an earlier psychosexual stage and engage in sex with a child. Best estimates are that fewer than 2 percent of priests have been sexually involved with prepubescent children (Plante 1999:172).

Researchers distinguish pedophiles from incest offenders and child molesters. Incest offenders sexually abuse a child or family member within his or her own family, while child molesters may sexually abuse a vulnerable child but often do not have an exclusive erotic preference for a child, while a pedophile does (Shriver et al. 2002).

Ephebophilia: Ephebophilia refers to the sexual attraction and arousal of adults to postpubescent or adolescent minors, arbitrarily designated between the ages fourteen through seventeen. Sexual activity with a minor thirteen or under is considered pedophilia. The cut-off age is set at seventeen since it is presumed that, legally, individuals who are eighteen and older can provide full consent to engage in sexual activity with an adult. Interestingly, Church law sets sixteen as the age at which an individual is capable of providing full consent, i.e., engaging in consensual sex. Curiously (American Psychiatric Association 2000), ephebophilia is considered both a grave moral failing and a legal offense—a felony, but *not* a DSM-IV psychiatric disorder, i.e., paraphilia. **Ephebophiles** are adults who are sexually attracted and aroused by postpubescent or adolescent minors. A clinically useful distinction can be made between fixated and regressed ephebophiles (Groth, Hobson, and Gary 1982). A *fixated ephebophile* is described as an individual whose primary sexual interest is in adolescents and rarely, if ever, engages in sex with other adults. These individuals are commonly involved with pornography and typically use alcohol or other drugs for their disinhibiting effect prior to engaging in sexual activity. They tend to be calculating rather than impulsive in their sexual exploits and use cunning, deceit and intimidation. There is growing consensus that these individuals are psychosexually immature and developmentally fixated. On the other hand, a *regressed ephebophile* is described as an individual whose primary sexual orientation is toward adults of the opposite sex. When under extreme stress such individuals can psychologically regress to an earlier psychosexual stage and engage in sex with an adolescent. Best estimates are that about 4–5 percent of priests have been sexually involved with postpubescent minors (Plante 1999:172).

NMBLA: Recent news reports note that some convicted clergy pedophilies have been members of or have advocated for NMBLA. What is NMBLA and its connection with pedophilia? The North American Man/Boy Love Association (NMBLA) is a group of gays who advocate sexual relations between adults and prepubescent minors, which they refer to as consensual "intergenerational relationships." Mainline gay and lesbian groups such as Human Rights Campaign Fund and the International Lesbian and Gay Association have distanced themselves from NMBLA because of its support of pedophilic activities. These groups also insist that NMBLA is not a gay organization and exclude it from Gay Pride Celebrations and other joint activities and publications (Shriver et al. 2002).

Impairment: Impairment refers to the inability to function in a ministerial capacity due to a debilitating medical, substance-related, or psychiatric condition or because of lack of "fit" between a predisposed minister and his or her assignment in a given diocese or province. Impairment tends to greatly reduce or prevent the minister from performing most or all of his or her ministry functions, and thus is global, i.e., terminal cancer or advanced, chronic alcoholism. Nevertheless, many impairments are amenable to treatment or remediation and some can actually be cured, i.e., phobias such as fear of heights or public speaking. Impairment can be distinguished from "professional distress" and "unfitness for ministry." In **professional distress** an actively functioning minister will occasionally experience decreased performance due to specific internal or external stressors. Professional distress can often be alleviated by addressing the specific stressors or response to them. On the other hand, in the situation of **unfitness for ministry,** individuals can often perform many or most aspects of their ministry sufficiently well without detection of their unfitness as is often the case in sexual misconduct or embezzlement of funds, at least in the early stages (Sperry 2000b). Nevertheless, because underlying ministry unfitness is a pattern of abusiveness as well as opaqueness of character and usually an unwillingness to participate or respond to efforts to address the unfitness, treatment or rededication efforts are often unsuccessful. Instead, removal from active ministry or even removal from the priesthood, i.e., laicization, are not uncommon remedies for unfitness. Whereas there are primarily physical and/or psychological factors involved in impairment, moral and characterological factors are more likely to be involved in unfitness for ministry. Fixated pedophilia and ephebophilia are obvious examples of unfitness for ministry.

Concluding Note

Despite a decidedly technical slant to some of these fifty-plus definitions and descriptions, these terms remain the coin of the realm in discussions about sexual issues in the Church. The reader will recognize the appearance of these terms in subsequent chapters. In most instances, the terms are defined in context. Where they are not, this chapter remains a ready resource.

References

American Psychiatric Association. (2000). *Diagnostic and Statistical Manual of Mental Disorders, Fourth Edition-Text Revision (DSM-IV-TR)*. Washington, D.C.: American Psychiatric Association.

Bagarozzi, D. (1999). "Marital Intimacy: Assessment and Clinical Considerations." In J. Carlson, and L. Sperry, eds., *The Intimate Couple*. New York: Brunner/Mazel. 66–83.

Bryant, C. (1999). "Psychological Treatment of Priest Sex Offenders." In T. Plante, ed., *Bless Me Father for I Have Sinned: Perspectives on Sexual Abuse Committed by Roman Catholic Priests*. Westport, Conn.: Praeger. 87–110.

Carnes, P. (1983). *Out of the Shadows. Understanding Sexual Addiction*. Minneapolis: CompCare.

Carnes, P. (1991). *Don't Call it Love. Recovery from Sexual Addiction*. New York: Bantam Books.

Cozzens, D. (2000). *The Changing Face of the Priesthood*. Collegeville: Liturgical Press.

Craig, G., and D. Baucom. (2002). *Human Development*. 9th ed. Upper Saddle River, N.J.: Prentice Hall.

DeLamater, J., and W. Friedrich. (2002). "Human Sexual Development." *Journal of Sex Research* 39 (1) 10–14.

Dynes, W. (1990). "Situational Homosexuality." In W. Dynes, ed., *Encyclopedia of Homosexuality*. New York: Garland Publishing. 2:1197–98.

Freud, S. (1924/1968). *A General Introduction to Psychoanalysis*. New York: Washington Square Press.

Friberg, N., and M. Laaser. (1998). *Before the Fall: Preventing Pastoral Sexual Abuse*. Collegeville: Liturgical Press.

Goergen, D. (1974). *The Sexual Celibate*. New York: Seabury.

Gonsiorek, J. (1999). "Forensic Psychological Evaluation in Clergy Abuse." In T. Plante, ed., *Bless Me Father for I Have Sinned: Perspectives on Sexual Abuse Committed by Roman Catholic Priests*. Westport, Conn.: Praeger. 27–58.

Groth, N., W. Hobson, and T. Gary. (1982). "The Child Molester: Clinical Observations." In J. Conte, and D. Shore, eds., *Social Work and Child Sexual Abuse*. New York: Haworth.

Kenel, M. (2002). "Impediments to Intimacy." *Human Development* 23 (1) 29–35.

Kennedy, E., and J. Heckler. (1971). *The Catholic Priest in the United States: Psychological Investigations*. Washington, D.C.: United States Catholic Conference.

King, B. (2002). *Human Sexuality Today*. Upper Saddle River, N.J.: Prentice-Hall.

Longres, J. (2000). *Human Behavior in the Social Environment*. 3rd ed. Itasca, Ill.: Peacock.

Nelson, J. (1988). *The Intimate Connection: Male Sexuality, Masculine Spirituality*. Philadelphia: Westminister.

Plante, T. (1999). Conclusion. "Sexual Abuse Committed by Roman Catholic Priests: Current Status, Future Objectives." In T. Plante, ed., *Bless Me Father for I Have Sinned: Perspectives on Sexual Abuse Committed by Roman Catholic Priests*. Westport, Conn.: Praeger. 171–77.

Shriver, S., C. Byer, L. Shainburg, and G. Falliano. (2002). *Dimensions of Human Sexuality*. Boston: McGraw Hill.

Sperry, L. (2000a). "The Abusive Personality in Ministry." *Human Development* 21 (3) 32–36.

Sperry, L. (2000b). *Ministry and Community: Recognizing, Healing and Preventing Ministry Impairment*. Collegeville: Liturgical Press.

Whitehead, E., and L. Whitehead. (1989). *A Sense of Sexuality: Christian Love and Intimacy*. New York: Doubleday.

Chapter 2

The Process of
Psychosexual Development

To the casual observer at the ordination of the diocesan seminary class of 1972, it appeared that three of its members had very much in common. Not only were the three friends the same age, but they shared similar interests and goals. No one would have predicted that some thirty years after ordination their lives would have taken such different paths. Today, Rev. Andy Sharff is on leave as a pastoral minister at the diocesan high school where he taught for the past eighteen years. Before that he had been a teacher there for ten years, and prior to that he was a pastoral associate at a large suburban parish. It shocked the community when he was recently charged with sexual impropriety involving three male adolescents. Rev. John Steffin served on a marriage tribunal in the diocese for the past twenty-six years. He had served as a pastoral associate for only one year before he was sent to pursue training in canon law. Rev. Jim Gilliam, on the other hand, is a pastor of one the largest parishes in the diocese, a post he has had for some twelve years. By all accounts he is quite effective and rather content in active parish ministry. Because of his enthusiasm and obvious talent demonstrated during his initial assignment as an associate pastor, he was assigned to a pastorate at a medium-size urban parish, and then later moved to other large parishes in the suburbs. A psychiatric evaluation today would have revealed that, of the three priests, only Rev. Gilliam had achieved a relatively high level of psychosexual development.

Psychosexual development is a term that is in the news a lot today. It is an often used but elusive term for which there is little consensus as to its meaning, its method of assessment or its clinical utility. Traditionally, psychosexual development was associated with the psychosexual stage model proposed by Freud nearly one hundred years ago. Interestingly, while sexual researchers and clinicians increasingly insist that the traditional concept is imprecise and reductionistic, has limited clinical value and should be replaced by more narrowly focused concepts such as *sexual development* or *gender identity development,* others in religious circles and the mass media routinely use the term *psychosexual development.* This widening rift, which is more than a matter of semantics, could be stemmed with a more precise, focused and clinically useful model of psychosexual development. This chapter presents one such model. It begins by briefly describing the traditional and reductionistic Freudian model, then presents a holistic and integrative model, and finally suggests its clinical applicability by analyzing the three opening case histories.

Psychosexual Development Yesterday

Generally speaking, psychosexual development refers to the evolving process of achieving an integrative sense of sexuality and sexual health. Prior to Freud, it was believed that only adolescents had the capacity for sexual responsivity. With his concept of *libido*—psychosexual energy—as the fundamental element of human experience, Freud contended that sexuality and the need for erotic gratification was present from the time of birth. He insisted that sexual development involved a continuous tension between biological drives, such as the id and libido, and social constraints. His psychosexual model describes a stage-by-stage process of the growth of human sexuality as it affects personality development. This process of psychosexual or libidinal development was understood to proceed through various stages, each associated with a specific libidinal or erogenous zone where libido would be focused.

Psychosexual development was conceptualized in terms of the *erogenous zone,* an area of the body that produces intense gratification when stimulated. The Freudian view of psychosexual development has been described in terms of five stages: oral, anal, phallic, latency, and genital. In this model, the process of personality development is uneventful for many individuals while it may become stunted or "fixated" for others. When development is fixated, individuals as adults continue to seek gratification in ways that are appropriate only to children. For example, Freud theorized that individuals who were over- or underfed as infants might become adults who immoderately eat, smoke, or drink, or are overly talkative.

Oral Stage (birth to age 1 1/2 years). Because the erogenous zone centers around the infant's lips and mouth, Freud called this the oral stage. Fixations associated with this stage presumably involve deriving gratification from eating, drinking, smoking, or talking.

Anal Stage (1 1/2 to 3 years). At this stage the erogenous zone shifts to the rectum and anus, at the time in which toilet training usually occurs. Here the child derives gratification and pleasure from the eliminatory function of defecation. Two fixations associated with this stage are anal retention and anal expulsion. Individuals are said to be "anal retentive" if they are considered to be "emotionally constipated," stubborn, or stingy. On the other hand, individuals are considered to be "anal explosive" if they have difficulty controlling thoughts and feelings, i.e., "emotional diarrhea."

Phallic Stage (3–6 years). The phallic stage comes about when the erogenous zone shifts to genital, where it presumably remains throughout life. During this stage Freud believed that boys develop lustful desires for their mothers but fail to act on these desires out of fear of becoming castrated by their fathers. This is called the Oedipus Complex. The resolution of this fear is for the boy to identify with his father and model the father's behavior, particularly regarding moral principles. This identification diminishes the likelihood of castration and develops the boy's superego. Freud described a similar phenomenon called the Electra Complex in which girls develop lustful feelings toward their fathers.

Latency Stage (6–12). Freud believed that during this time frame sexual impulses and urges were latent, dormant, or temporarily sublimated in hobbies, school activities, and developing same-sex friendships. Accordingly, he designated this as a stage of latency. Initially, he believed that sexual development was essentially completed at this stage. Later, the importance of adolescent sexuality was recognized and further described.

Genital Stage (Age 12 onward). With the onset of adolescence and the resurgence of sexual impulses in the genital region, the true genital stage, called by some the puberty phase, began. During this stage secondary sexual characteristics such as increased breast development and pubic hair are noted. Freud believed that sexual energy that was pressing for expression could be partially satisfied through socially acceptable substitutes in adolescence and later through a mature, intimate adult relationship with a person of the opposite sex. The mark of mental health for such an adult would be in finding satisfaction in work and love, wherein love becomes an acceptable outlet for sublimating id impulses.

This process could unfold in a normal or uneventful fashion in some individuals, while it can be stunted or "fixated" in others. For Freud, "normal psychosexual development means internalizing the norms and traditions of society, identifying with the same-sex parent, and fulfilling sexual gratification through genital/genital contact with a member of the opposite sex" (Longres 2000:431). Not surprisingly, some find this conclusion untenable.

Freud's psychosexual stage model has been criticized on several grounds. First, it is criticized for being *androcentric,* i.e., male-centered or -dominated, and *homophobic,* i.e., an irrational fear of or ideological bias against homosexuals or homosexuality. Some question Freud's basic assumption that sexual capacity is a primordial biological drive, i.e., libido, that is directly expressed in psychosocial and social behaviors and is unmediated by cognitions or sociocultural influences. Instead, they contend that sexuality is primarily a learned, social behavior that is "constructed" or scripted differently across cultures.

Second, Freud's model has also been criticized as being *reductionistic,* i.e., focusing primarily on the biological-psychological aspect of libido. Third, neither research nor the experience of countless generations of celibates supports the contention that sexuality is an intense, high-pressure drive that impels an individual to seek physical sexual gratification directly or indirectly. Rather, there are several situations in which reduced sexual activity or the vow of celibacy is undertaken with little evidence that libido has shifted to compensate in some other sphere of life.

An Integrative Model of Psychosexual Development

Unlike Freud's reductionistic model which is based on a single developmental line, a more integrative model would account for other lines of human development that normally evolve over the course of life. The integrative model proposed in this chapter accounts for four lines of development. It also specifies five age-related stages ranging from birth through middle adulthood reflecting the process of achieving an integrative sense of self and sexuality. At the present time there is an insufficient research basis for more than speculating on later adulthood thus, this stage is not included. Underlying this model are eight basic premises which are articulated in the next section. Then, seven predisposing factors are described as well as several other developmental factors associated with the five stages.

Some Basic Premises

This book is based on eight premises or assumptions. These interrelated premises provide a conceptual basis for understanding both the integrative model of psychosexual development and related sexual dynamics and issues and also for utilizing this knowledge for making informed decisions about some major issues facing the Church today.

Sexuality is more than sex. The term sex has two common designations, the biological status based on the appearance of genitals—male or female—and its genital expression or behavior, i.e., "we had sex." The term sexuality encompasses both sex, i.e., who we are and what we think, feel, and do sexually, as well as the meanings given to sex. According to Evelyn and James Whitehead, sexuality is "What our body means to us, how we understand ourself as a woman or as a man, the way we feel comfortable in expressing affection—these are part of our sexuality. . . . In this broadest sense, sexuality is how we make sex significant" (Whitehead and Whitehead 1989:45). Sexuality usually involves physical indications of caring and concern such as touching with or without genital expression or related sexual activities or practices.

Asexuality is a sexual orientation. Traditionally, three sexual orientations have been described: heterosexual, homosexual, and bisexual. Unfortunately, there are a sizeable number of ministry personnel who are not well represented by these categories. That is probably because the traditional model of orientation is premised on the nature of the sexual attraction experienced. While useful, this model does not account for those individuals who deny or are uncertain of such attraction, i.e., asexuality. An alternate model of sexual orientation has been described by Storms (1981). In this model, sexual orientation is based on the type, extent, and frequency of sexual fantasies and arousal. Four types of arousal are noted which translate into four orientations. Accordingly, the heterosexual orientation refers to arousal involving persons of the opposite sex, the homosexual orientation involves arousal by the same sex, and bisexual involves arousal by either sex. The fourth orientation is designated as asexual, in which there is no arousal to either sex.

Psychosexual development is a key facet of human development. In recent years it has become more clear that sexual development is not a form of development separate or independent of other forms of development. Rather, sexual development occurs within the context of human development processes, and it includes biological, psychological, social-cultural, and spiritual dimensions or lines of development. Here, we will follow the common convention of combining the social and cultural dimensions and referring to them simply as the "social" line of development.

The trajectory of psychosexual development is influenced by several predisposing factors. Research and clinical observation reveal that, in addition to early childhood through adulthood experiences and developmental challenges, there are a number of environmental, pregnancy-related, and perinatal, i.e., around the time of birth, influences that appear to significantly impact sexual development. These include testosterone levels, birth complications, and family attitudes about sexuality, to name three. Thus, an adequate understanding of psychosexual development should include such predisposing factors, which are distinguishable from developmental factors, i.e., factors associated with childhood, adolescence, and adulthood.

Because of the complexity of the process of human development, an integrative model of development is essential. Neither a biological, nor a psychological model—such as Freud's theory of psychosexual development—nor a spiritual model, nor even a social model provides an adequate understanding and explanation of the complexity of sexual development, much less of the complex process of human development. Not even composite models such as Erikson's stages theory, which combines both psychological and social dimensions, is sufficient. However, an integrative and nonreductionistic model, which we call the "biopsychosociospiritual model," appears to offer a more comprehensive and holistic understanding of the development process.

The developmental endpoint of psychosexual development, and indeed all of human development, is union. In *The Changing*

Face of the Priesthood, Donald Cozzens (2000) describes intimacy and transcendence as the dual innate longings or drives which inevitably lead an individual ultimately to union with God. He defines intimacy as the experience of union with another and transcendence as union with creation, with the combination of intimacy and transcendence leading ultimately with God. In the psychological literature, two core concepts of human development are autonomy and belonging or relationship. Life reflects an ongoing tension between these two polar dimensions. Transcendence and mature intimacy reflect an energizing balance between autonomy and relationship, which allows individuals to transcend their own self-interest to experience union with creation and God. It is proposed then that the expected endpoint of all the lines of human development is a mature and integrated sense of union or intimacy which is reflected in wholeness and holiness. In addition, it presupposed that there is an increasing convergence of each of the four principal lines of development—biological, psychological, social, and spiritual—as the process of human development evolves.

Accordingly, we can describe the ultimate endpoint of the biological line as union with another individual and integrated sexual functioning or "sexual health" as it is more commonly known. Possibly, sexual exploration, which characterizes at least the first three stages of development, is best understood as a means of seeking union. The ultimate endpoint of the psychological line of development would be union with self, i.e., a cohesive, integrated sense of self including a healthy sexual identity. Likewise, the ultimate endpoint of the social line of development would be union with other persons, i.e., mature relational functioning which presupposes a high degree of integration in the biological and psychological developmental lines. And, finally, the ultimate endpoint of the spiritual line of development would be union with God, the ultimate of intimacy and transcendence.

The relationship between autonomy and intimacy is the basic dynamic in psychosexual development. Autonomy and related concepts such as separation–individuation and independence, are the polar opposites of intimacy and its related concepts of union, dependence, belongingness, attachment, and relationship. The process of healthy development involves progressively increasing both autonomy and intimacy—called interdependence—while also maintaining a healthy tension and balance between the two. Separation–individuation is an ongoing process which begins as the infant gradually differentiates self from the mother in order to achieve some degree of autonomy developmental stages. Seven orienting factors can be described along with some probable or actual dysfunctional influences.

Pregnancy and Birth Experience. Parental attitudes toward pregnancy can subsequently influence a child's overall health and sense of self-efficacy and self-confidence. To the extent to which individuals sense and internalize they were unwanted or that their parents were ambivalent about their birth, these individuals may be less certain of themselves or may believe they must prove their worth or otherwise act out in response. Health problems, e.g., bacterial infections, or toxic influences, e.g., maternal use of drugs or serious illness, can impair normal prenatal development, as can problems associated with the birth process itself, e.g., prematurity, cesarean delivery, postpartum depression, etc. While such prenatal and birth experiences do not inevitably derail the normal process of development, they can and often do negatively impact attitudes and behavior as well as the health status of adults.

Temperament and Personality. Temperament refers to inborn tendencies of an individual to respond and behave in characteristic ways and patterns that are evident from birth. For example, while some infants are quite sensitive to light and loud sounds, others are not, and while some are calm and placid, others can be very active or very fussy. Three main temperament patterns or styles have been observed in infants: *easy* (usually predictable and in a good mood), *slow to warm* (more likely to be resistant to attention and moody), and *difficult* (typically unpredictable and with irritable moods) (Thomas and Chess 1977). A child's temperament is reflected in his or her personality style as an adult, which is to say that adult patterns such as optimism and consistency of effort are more common in individuals with easy temperaments, with negativity and suspiciousness associated with the "difficult" temperament, and passivity and overdependency with the "slow to warm up" temperament.

Hormonal Makeup. Hormones can greatly influence the rate and extent of biological processes as well as the extent and intensity of psychological processes. Levels of the hormone testosterone are associated with both sexual desire and sexual response. Individuals with high levels of testosterone can have spontaneous sex thoughts and fantasies, are early aroused, and desire sex often. On the other hand, those with low levels have little or no sexual fantasy, desire, or arousal. These hormonal levels appear to be constant from the time of birth, suggesting that sexual desire and arousal are relatively constant throughout life unless modified by medication or medical condition. Similarly, the hormone oxytocin has been shown to influence attachment behaviors in both infants and adults (Crenshaw 1996). Thus, higher levels are related to increased degrees of attachment while lower levels are associated with lesser degrees of attachment.

Attachment Styles. Attachment refers to the emotional bond that develops between child and parent or caregiver and subsequently influences the child's capacity to form mature intimate relationships in adulthood. It is an inborn system of the brain that influences and organizes motivational, emotional, and memory process that involve caregivers. The impact of the process of attachment on development cannot be underestimated since the "patterning and organization of attachment relationships during infancy is associated with characteristic processes of emotional regulation, social relatedness, access to autobiographical memory, and the development of self-reflection and narrative" (Siegel 1999:67).

Distinct patterns or styles of attachment can be described. When the style of attachment is characterized by emotional interdependence, trust, and mutual feelings, it is called a "secure" style. As adults, individuals with secure styles exhibit more physical and emotional resilience as compared to those with insecure styles. That is to say, they are less vulnerable to stressors and, consequently, are less likely to experience health problems, depression, anxiety, substance abuse, or sexual and other psychiatric disorders. On the other hand, vulnerability is associated with "insecure" styles, i.e., attachment styles characterized by inconsistency or emotional unavailability. Two insecure styles are briefly noted: avoidant and anxious (Ainsworth et al. 1978).

The avoidant style of attachment is characterized by a fear of closeness, intimacy, and commitment. That is, adults with this style prefer to maintain interpersonal distance (Karen 1994). Their parents were likely to have been cold, distant, and rejecting. Interestingly, individuals with such an avoidant attachment style appear to have low sexual desire which likely reflects their early relational experiences, as with their parents. In addition, such individuals tend to deny their own feelings as well as their personal needs. Unfortunately, when these individuals were screened for the priesthood, they were considered ideal candidates for ordination because neither celibacy nor chastity seemed to be problems or concerns for them. This attachment style can be noted in some ministers whose behavior suggests hyposexuality, i.e., a sexual orientation called "asexuality."

Adult relationships with the anxious/ambivalent style, sometimes called the preoccupied style, are characterized by intensity and chaos. Individuals with this style tend to be highly emotionally involved with others, particularly significant others, sometimes to the point of obsession (Karen 1994). Sometimes others are viewed as unresponsive, unreliable, or unavailable, which can trigger anger and anxiety in those with this style. As children these individuals were found to have had inconsistent parenting. This attachment style may be observed in some ministers whose behavior suggests hypersexuality, i.e., sexual preoccupation and/or compulsivity, or sexual acting-out behavior.

Level of Family Competence and Style. Family competence is the technical designation for the level of functioning of a given family. Highly competent—healthy and mature—families show warmth, respect, intimacy, and humor along with the capacity to negotiate difficulties and maintain appropriate boundaries and have clear boundaries. Families with low competence—less healthy and immature—have problematic boundaries, confused communication, and either overcontrol family members or provide no structure or consistency (Beavers and Hampson 1990). Family style refers to the manner in which families relate to one another. For example, in the enmeshed or overly engaged style, families emphasize extreme dependency as well as closeness, and sameness in how family members think, feel, and act. On the other hand, disengaged style families emphasize extreme independence, which is reflected in relatively little cohesion and consistency in how family members relate to each other (Beavers and Hampson 1990). Healthier families tend to have a high level of competence and a style that is interdependent, i.e., blends both the engaged and disengaged styles. Needless to say, sexually problematic ministers often come from problematic families.

Family Attitudes Toward Intimacy and Sexuality. Parental attitudes toward intimacy and sexuality tend to be adopted by children. Thus, children whose parents hold reasonably healthy attitudes are less likely to have negative or ambivalent attitudes toward marriage and intimacy. Consequently, they are also less likely to experience unhealthy shame and guilt about sex and sexuality (DeLamater and Friedrich 2002).

History of Early Abuse or Neglect. A history of verbal, emotional, physical, spiritual, and/or sexual abuse in childhood or adolescence can significantly impact an individual's overall biopsychosocial and spiritual development. Research increasingly demonstrates that early abuse negatively impacts normal brain development. It also suggests that adults who were emotionally and sexually abused as minors have a higher probability of sexually abusing minors than adults without such experience of early abuse (Rossetti 1990).

Having three or more potential or actual indicators of dysfunction on these orienting factors does not necessarily indicate that an individual will have difficulties or is unfit for ministry. But it might suggest that effective functioning will take considerable effort or that psychotherapy may be helpful or necessary.

Factors and Dysfunction by Developmental Stage

Each stage of human development provides individuals with an opportunity to grow or differentiate functioning to a higher degree than the previous stage. Specific developmental tasks are noted for each stage. These tasks challenge the individual to proceed further along a given developmental line, be it biological, psychological, or social. Irrespective of the developmental line, tasks tend to be of two types: personal and relational. Failure to deal adequately with these tasks results in either an overdeveloped or hypersexual response, or an underdeveloped or hyposexual response. Both forms are referred to by some as a "stunting," "arresting," or "fixating" of development that has both an immediate effect and also impacts functioning at a later stage or stages of development, typically late adolescence, or early or middle adulthood. This delayed impact is referred to here as "expected resulting adult sexual dysfunction." Nevertheless, these behaviors can be understood as inappropriate efforts to achieve some measure of union with another.

Childhood Stage: (ages 0–7)

Research confirms that the capacity for sexual responding is present from birth (DeLamater and Friedrich 2002). Biologically, the infant, and later the child, begins to actualize this capacity by exploring his or her sexuality at first openly and then discreetly as the child becomes aware of family and societal norms governing sexual expression. Psychologically, the child begins to develop a sense of trust and experiences other people and the world as positive and consistent, largely because of an already developing secure attachment style. Furthermore, the child begins to learn to differentiate self from others and to cope with the anxiety and uncertainty associated with early separation–individuation experiences. This coping is accomplished in a number of ways, most notably by learning to self-soothe early on through finger-sucking and later with transitional objects such as a favorite blanket or stuffed animal that the child associates with safety and security, such as parents or caregivers. Socially, the child begins to learn adult roles and expected behaviors through modeling. The child then practices these gender roles and behaviors by "playing house." By age three, a gender identity will begin being expressed. Typically, the child will form a "best friend" relationship in which he or she can risk sharing secrets and personal dreams with another, usually a child of similar age and same sex, without being criticized or having the secret "breached." Spiritually, it has been suggested that *in utero* the child experiences union and following birth clings to the mother or caregiver to recapture that sense of union by merging or sharing in the mother's sense of self. As the process of separation–individuation begins, the child appears to form a God-image or divine internal representation of his or her union with God as the child reflects on the attachment with parents. That is, a secure and caring paternal attachment tends to be reflected in a secure and caring image of God, while an insecure attachment with uncaring parents with a negative view of sexuality is reflected in an uncaring and/or guilt-inducing image of God. The basic personal task at this stage is self-soothing, while the basic relational task is to form a concept of committed, long-term relationships like marriage and to practice gender roles.

Expected resulting adult sexual dysfunction at this stage usually includes an overdeveloped or hypersexual response such as sexual preoccupation and fantasies, or the undeveloped or hyposexual response called asexuality, i.e., little or no sexual arousal or desire.

Preadolescence Stage (ages 8–12)

At this stage children tend to congregate and play in separate or homosocial groups, i.e., girls separated from the boys (DeLamater and Friedrich 2002). Such a separation means that sexual exploration at this stage tends to involve individuals of the same gender. Later in this stage children also begin experiencing the onset of hormonal changes, secondary sex characteristics, and feelings of sexual attraction. Psychologically, the children in this stage also begin to deal with body-image changes and have experiences which foster or undermine their sense of self-mastery. Later in this stage, involvement in heterosexual parties and group dating begin to occur. Spiritually, individuals at this stage tend to incorporate religious attitudes and prohibitions about sexuality into their previously assimilated familial and social norms and prohibitions, and this may be reflected in their God-image. The result is that guilt feelings and shame may intensify. The basic personal task at this stage is to develop an increasing sense of self-mastery which includes self-discipline and perseverance, while the basic relational task is to begin forming the capacity to maintain close relationships.

Expected resulting adult sexual dysfunction at this stage typically includes overdeveloped or hypersexual behaviors such as pedophilia, child pornography, compulsive masturbation, or other paraphilias. An undeveloped or hyposexual response may include superficial sexual relating, i.e., relating to other-sex adults in a markedly superficial, overly solicitous, or ambivalent manner (Cavanagh 1983).

Adolescence Stage (ages 13–19)

Puberty is the early part of adolescence during which the individual becomes functionally capable of reproduction. A hormonal surge during puberty leads to heightened sexual interest. For most individuals, sexual experiences begin during this stage. These include sexual fantasies and genital exploration, e.g., masturbation, petting, intercourse, etc. The majority of adolescents begin to masturbate at least occasionally, and approximately 50 percent experiment with heterosexual intercourse, while between 5–10 percent of males and 6 percent of females report having sexual experiences with a person of the same sex (DeLamater and Friedrich 2002). Many boys will experience their first nocturnal emission in early adolescence. This experience may be confusing or pleasurable and may include sexual fantasies. Psychologically, the adolescent begins to develop a stable sense of self and begins constellating a personal identity that includes a sexual identity and sexual orientation. Following this period of exploration, individuals become more comfortable with and in control of their sexuality and clearer about their orientation. On the other hand, because of social pressures, homosexually oriented individuals may not resolve their orientation issues until the stage of early adulthood. Socially, the adolescent begins to relate with a respect for boundaries and equality toward others irrespective of age, gender, or ethnicity. Spiritually, as the adolescent's capacity for abstract thought and analysis emerges, previously accepted religious beliefs may be questioned and discarded. At the same time the adolescent may more deeply experience a longing and desire for transcendent experiences which can be satisfied to some extent with music and experimentation with drugs and mind-altering substances. Through experimentation the adolescent may experience transcendence in sexual orgasm, possibly enhanced by drugs or other disinhibiting substances, which may be a source of guilt or great delight. The basic personal task at this stage is to develop a stable sense of self in the context of conflict and social influences, while basic relational task is to establish and maintain a basic level of emotional intimacy (DeLamater and Friedrich 2002). Emotional intimacy involves communicating and sharing both positive and negative feelings with another, usually a close friend or friends. Needless to say, such sharing is not without considerable risk of being teased, criticized, or having very personal information broadcast to others. Adolescents who have not had a best friend in childhood are somewhat at a disadvantage and may not even attempt such sharing.

The first indications of sexual deviancy may appear at this stage. Expected resulting adult sexual dysfunction at this stage typically includes such excessive or hypersexual behaviors as ephebophilia, adolescent pornography, and compulsive masturbation; Don Juanism, i.e., achieving sexual conquests with adult females; or other paraphilias. Just as individuals with excessive sexual involvement at this stage can have sexual problems later, so too can those individuals with limited sexual curiosity or fantasies, or sexual repression.

Early Adulthood Stage (ages 20–39)

Throughout this stage, the individual has the opportunity to further develop sexual maturity. Biologically, the young adult begins to engage a sexual lifestyle, i.e., celibacy, commitment to marriage, or promiscuity. Psychologically, the young adult begins to further establish a professional identity and competence and to undertake a career path compatible with his or her interests and talents (DeLamater and Friedrich 2002). An additional development task is to increase the capacity for critical reflection that will foster the completion of university education and success in subsequent employment. During this period individuals are also challenged to develop their capacity for critical social consciousness, which is to say they become increasingly aware of the impact of institutions and social sin on individuals, particularly the poor and marginalized (Sperry 2001). Not surprisingly, the more the individual is overly focused on career, the greater likelihood of delaying development of this capacity. Socially, the young adult begins to deepen commitments to relationships and to balance competition/cooperation. Spiritually, the individual may find his or her image of God shifting to a healthier, more life-giving, and more inclusive image, i.e., God can be masculine and feminine, weak and strong, etc., or the image can remain the same. Such individuals may get in closer touch with their deepest desires or longings for unity, taking the form of both transcendence and intimacy. Finding and maintaining a close, committed friendship can satisfy much of this desire for intimacy, while becoming more in touch with nature may help satisfy the desire for transcendence. It is not that prayer is not a part of the young adult's life but rather that it has a lower priority or perceived value. The basic personal task at this stage is to further integrate or constellate the various facets of self-identity—personal, professional, and social—while the basic relational task is to increase the communication and empathic responding in intimate relationships (DeLamater and Friedrich 2002). This is often a major challenge for males who have overidentified with the masculine function.

Sexual dysfunction at this stage typically includes problems with sexual desire or sexual performance. It can include the full range of hypersexual behaviors noted above, as well as the hyposexual ones.

Middle Adulthood Stage (ages 40–55)

Biologically, adults are challenged to deal with andropause, the male equivalent of menopause, and its meaning and consequences for their lives. Decreases in sexual desire, arousal, and performance, less energy, longer healing time after illnesses and injuries, loss of muscle mass, and associated signs of aging are painful realities and insults to an individual's sense of self and self-esteem. A major challenge is to accept these physical changes as a call to focus on one's interior life while maintaining a health lifestyle (DeLamater and Friedrich 2002). Psychologically, the major challenge at this stage is to become more fully the persons they were meant to be by becoming more single-minded, more loving and caring, and more whole. It means achieving better balance between autonomy and intimacy and between self-interest and self-surrender. Socially, the adult engages in generative behaviors, i.e., focuses on giving back to the community with volunteer activities, etc. Spiritually, the task is to develop spiritual intimacy. Individuals at this stage can respond to the dual desire and longing for intimacy and transcendence by becoming more sensitive to relationships through putting others' needs and interests first and by becoming more meditative and prayerful. Individuals in this stage are more attracted to centering prayer and related forms of meditation than in previous stages. The basic personal task at this stage is to become more centered and balanced, while the basic relational task at this stage is to reconfirm one's basic sexual lifestyle option. For most priests, this is celibacy, that is, if they follow an integrative developmental trajectory.

Sexual dysfunction at this stage typically includes problems with sexual desire or sexual performance. It can include the full range of hypersexual behaviors noted above, as well as the hyposexual ones. Also, unique to this stage is the experience of social isolation, loneliness, and depression that often reflects a nonintegrative sense of sexuality.

Table 2-1 offers a summary of these various developmental factors, tasks, and resultant sexual issues in adulthood.

Table 2-1: Sexual Development: Tasks and Dysfunction

Stage	*Stage-Specific Biopsychosociospiritual Developmental Factors and Basic Personal and Relational Tasks*	*Resulting Sexual Issues in Adulthood*
Predisposing (prenatal to postnatal)	**(B)** problematic pregnancy or birth complications; difficult temperament and/or poor mother-infant "fit"; abnormal hormone levels, e.g., testosterone **(P)** insecure attachment style **(S)** low family functioning and/or overly enmeshed or disengaged; early abuse or neglect history; **(Sp)** overly negative or permissive family attitudes re: sex and religion	establishes the vulnerability for subsequent sexual problems and amplifies sexual, self, and relational problems and concerns
Childhood (0–7)	**(B)** explore their sexuality at first openly and then discreetly, i.e., "play doctor"; **(P)** develop trust; learn to self-soothe; deal with early separation–individuation experiences; **(S)** learn and practice adult roles by "playing house," begin establishing a gender identity around age 3; have best friend; **(Sp)** develop God-image reflecting attachment to their parents **Basic Personal Task:** learn to self-soothe **Basic Relational Task:** form concept of marriage and long-term relationships, and practice gender roles	sexual preoccupation and fantasies **asexuality**

Stage (cont.)	Stage-Specific Developmental (cont.)	Sexual Issues (cont.)
Preadolescence (8–12)	**(B)** engage in homosocial sexual exploration; experience onset of hormonal changes, secondary sex characteristics, and feelings of sexual attraction **(P)** deal with body-image changes; experience self-mastery **(S)** engage in homosocial play and later heterosexual parties and group dating **(Sp)** incorporate religious norms about sexuality into their God-image and personal behavior **Basic Personal Task:** develop an increasing sense of self-mastery that includes self-discipline and perseverance **Basic Relational Task:** begin forming capacity to maintain close relationships	superficial sexual relating; **pedophilia;** child pornography; compulsive masturbation; other paraphilias
Adolescence (13–19)	**(B)** experience sexual fantasies and genital exploration such as masturbation, petting, intercourse, etc. **(P)** develop a stable sense of self and begin constellating a personal identity that includes a sexual identity and sexual orientation; capacity for self-directedness and responsibility, cooperation and self-transcendence **(S)** relate to others with a respect for boundaries and equality irrespective of age, gender, ethnicity **(Sp)** seek to satisfy deep longing for the transcendent in music, drugs, or spiritual experience; critical reappraisal of previous religious beliefs **Basic Personal Task:** develop a stable sense of self in the context of conflict and social influences **Basic Relational Task:** learn to maintain emotional intimacy	**ephebophilia;** adolescent pornography; compulsive masturbation; Don Juanism/sexual conquests; other paraphilias

Stage (cont.)	Stage-Specific Developmental (cont.)	Sexual Issues (cont.)
Early Adulthood (20–39)	**(B)** forge sexual lifestyle, e.g., celibacy or monogamous marriage **(P)** further establish a professional identity and/or career path; develop critical reflection and a critical social consciousness; **(S)** deepen commitments to relationships; balance competition/cooperation **(Sp)** experience transcendence in close, committed friendship and being more in touch with nature **Basic Personal Task:** integrate professional identity into self-identity **Basic Relational Task:** develop effective communication in intimate relationships	the full range of hypersexual and hyposexual behaviors noted above, as well as problems with sexual desire or sexual performance
Mid-Adulthood (40–55)	**(B)** deal with andropause/menopause and its meaning/consequences **(P)** balance self-interest with self-surrender; become more centered/whole **(S)** engage in generative behaviors, i.e., focus on giving back to community with volunteer activities, etc. **(Sp)** develop deeper spiritual intimacy re: prayer and centeredness **Basic Personal Task:** become more centered and balanced **Basic Relational Task:** reconfirm sexual lifestyle option, i.e., celibacy	same as early adulthood; plus social isolation, loneliness, and depression reflective of a nonintegrative sexuality

Key: **B = biological factor(s)**
      P = psychological factor(s)
      S = social factor(s)
      Sp=spiritual factor(s)

Psychosexual Development in Three Priests

What is the practical significance, if any, of this integrative model? Let's apply the model to the three cases described at the beginning of this chapter by noting relevant predisposing and developmental factors that are reflected in the development path or trajectory for each of these men from birth through the present time in their priestly ministries.

Rev. Jim Gilliam

From the time Mrs. Gilliam's pregnancy was confirmed by her physician, Jim was loved and cherished by his parents. That pregnancy and birth were uneventful, and his "easy" temperament and secure bonding with his mother seemed to facilitate his becoming the center of his parent's affection and attention. Furthermore, he was their firstborn son. Their attitudes toward intimacy and sexuality were positive, and when it was appropriate, Jim's father discussed sex and sexual awakening with him. Jim was on target for all his biological and psychological developmental milestones. His gender identity as masculine was evident at age three. He played with neighborhood children, becoming a leader of sorts, and had a best friend beginning at age five. In his middle-school years he related with relative ease with both boys and girls, attending parties and engaging in group dating starting in his second year of high school. He reported sexual fantasies involving girls his age when he was twelve and engaged in occasional masturbation starting at age thirteen. If a hormonal assay had been available it would have likely indicated normal testosterone levels. He was an honor student, active in school sports, continued to date through high school, and was a class leader. There was a certain charm, transparency, and sensitivity about him that made it easy for others, both students and faculty, to like him and enjoy his company. By his late teens his sexual orientation and identity were clearly heterosexual, and while he had some concerns about celibacy, he was pretty sure he wanted to be a priest like his paternal uncle. Accordingly, he entered the diocesan minor seminary after high school. Looking back, it was evident that he was able to reasonably manage physical and emotional intimacy and had made a reasonably informed decision about the sexual option of celibacy prior to his ordination. Throughout his parish ministry he was considered an effective sacramental minister and a balanced pastoral administrator. Furthermore, he was well liked by his parishioners. The late 1970s and early

1980s were a difficult time for him as some of his closest priest colleagues left to marry and raise families. During this period of soul-searching he reaffirmed his commitment to celibacy. After this "dark night" he seemed to experience renewed energy and passion for his pastoral responsibilities.

Rev. John Steffin

While John Steffin's pregnancy and birth were uneventful, his parents were ambivalent about the pregnancy. At the time, his parents were farmers who were financially strained by a recent drought and a downturn in the economy. John's "slow to warm" temperament was not a good "fit" for his mother's impatience and emotional distancing. Needless to say, the avoidant attachment style that characterized the bond between John and his mother was further reinforced by the social isolation John experienced as a child. The farm was in a remote rural area and consequently John had no regular playmates in his first six years of life. When the farm failed, the family moved to the city where his father took a factory job, and John attended first grade at a Catholic school. While the first-grade teacher was a warm and inclusive person, John was one of thirty-five students in the class. Furthermore, John's seeming reluctance to join in playground activities with his peers further accentuated his separateness. Needless to say, he was teased as "the hick from the sticks." This teasing was very hurtful to John, and rather than strike back verbally or by fighting, he retreated to the safety of the role of "book worm" and "brain" in the class. His parents' attitudes toward sex were decidedly negative, and at age seven when John's mother caught him in his room stimulating his penis, she rebuked him saying he should "never do such an evil thing again." John was deeply shamed by this experience and obeyed her, i.e., he never masturbated or engaged in any other sexual exploration again. John's father never thought to talk to his son about sex and sexuality, and because there was no sex education in schools at that time, his only knowledge of sex came from a book article he read for a class report. Nevertheless, he did identify rather strongly with his father, reflected by John's early gender identity as masculine. He also identified with a highly intelligent priest on the seminary faculty who was a weekend associate at the family's parish. It was this priest who would eventually encourage John to enter the seminary after graduation from high school. In his middle-school years John developed a friendship with two other boys who were similarly intellectually inclined and nonathletic. Not surprisingly, John graduated as valedictorian of his class. He never dated in high school and could not recall ever having sexual fantasies involving either sex or engaging in sexual behaviors. Had a hormonal assay been available, it would have likely indicated low testosterone levels. When John announced his decision to enter the minor seminary that fall, his mother was overjoyed, saying it was the happiest day of her life. While John knew his parents were practicing Catholics, his mother had never communicated her wish that John would become a priest and "bring down blessings on this family." John's days in the seminary were idyllic. He excelled in classes and easily tolerated the strict regimen of the minor seminary life in the 1960s. This is not to say that John was always pleasant and easygoing; on the contrary, his irritability and moodiness were quite evident. Nevertheless, while others could not understand the prohibition against "particular friendships," John was content to spend time during breaks discussing ideas with some of his more intellectually oriented peers. He imaged his life as a priest on the seminary faculty or in some specialized role such as a tribunal, although he realized that he would have to spend some time "on the line" in a parish assignment, at least for a while. Even though the major seminary formation team had some concerns about John's apparent shyness, they were impressed with his intellectual capability—he was the top student in his class—and the fact that he had no obvious issues about sexuality nor celibacy. Neither John nor his bishop realized how difficult his first parish assignment would be. While John could preach adequately, he often came across to parishioners who tried to talk with him as a cold, uncaring, and unconcerned cleric. Others viewed him as irritable, moody, and even downright inhospitable. During this early postconciliar era when there were high expectations for collaboration between priests and laity, John's attitude toward the newly elected parish council was highly critical and disparaging. Parishioners were upset, and the pastor, who had high hopes for both John and the prospects of having an active parish council, was very discouraged. Furthermore, John was an absolute failure in his role with his youth ministry responsibilities. After eight months in that assignment, the pastor urgently requested that John be removed as soon as possible. While he was scheduled for graduate study in two more years, the diocese moved up the time line and arranged for that assignment to begin at the end of that assignment year.

Rev. Andy Sharff

Mrs. Sharff was thrilled to hear she was pregnant. While her husband was seldom home because of business, he too looked forward to beginning a family. Her pregnancy was somewhat problematic and he was born four weeks prematurely, probably because of Mrs. Sharff's drug and alcohol usage throughout pregnancy. Andy's "difficult" temperament was not a particularly good "fit" for his mother who was quite anxious and impatient. While she really wanted to give Andy all her love and concern, her anxiety and inconsistent efforts were reflected in the anxious-ambivalent attachment style that developed between them. Parental attitudes toward both sexuality and drug use were quite liberal. Both his parents drank regularly, and his mother used a variety of prescription "uppers" and "downers." As a youngster, Andy was allowed to play with other children but was regularly told to "keep family business to yourself," which Andy assumed meant he shouldn't talk about his parents' drinking and arguments or the men that visited his mother when his father was away on business. Andy complied. Even when he was fondled on several occasions by one of these men just before he turned thirteen, he told no one. Although initially frightened, he immensely enjoyed the experience and afterwards began to masturbate once or more a day thereafter. While he knew most of the kids in the area, he never really had a best friend. In his middle-school years he did attend some mixed parties and engaged in group dating, but his attraction was more toward boys. From his early adolescence Andy recalled overhearing his parents fighting about money matters and their infidelities. The only sexual education and advice his father gave him was to "use protection and you'll never have to worry." While Andy was angry that his father knew so little about him and his sexual attraction, he could not talk to his father about his concerns. He recalled sexual fantasies involving boys his age when he was twelve. While he had masturbated occasionally since age nine, he now masturbated almost daily starting at age thirteen. He also experienced a nagging sense of guilt over both his masturbation and the sexual molestation that was reinforced by the sexual ethics he learned in his Catholic elementary and high-school religion classes. If a hormonal assay had been available it would have likely indicated high testosterone levels. Although he had high intellectual capabilities, he was only an average student. He was very active in all school sports and enjoyed hanging around the locker room with his teammates. Still, he had time for student council activities and, largely due to his popularity rather than any particular talents or accomplishments, he was elected student council president in his senior year. By his late teens his sexual orientation and identity seemed to be primarily homosexual with sexual fantasies and arousal primarily involving younger adolescent males. Uncertain about his future and confused about his sexuality, he was easily recruited into the diocesan seminary. His mother, while surprised since Andy had never mentioned any such interest, was pleased. To the screening committee Andy appeared to be a bright, handsome young male who was socially adept. Today, a detailed inquiry would have disclosed that Andy had only a limited capacity for mature intimate relationships and his psychosexual development was significantly arrested. When he learned he was admitted he breathed a sigh of relief for now he believed he could control his sexual urges by giving himself fully to God and to God's work. He felt grateful to be in a secure environment for the first time in his life, and easily rose to be one of the top students in his class. While he had some attraction to his fellow seminarians, his sexual fantasies primarily involved young adolescent boys. Once he summoned the courage to talk about his sexual desires to his spiritual director. The only advice he was given was "to pray and masturbate, if you have to, and then leave the rest to God." His first ministry assignment was to a parish. After a few years it became apparent to the clergy personnel board that Andy had a talent for relating to youth, and so he was subsequently assigned to teach at one of the diocese's co-ed high schools. For the first fifteen or so years he had little difficulty with sexual matters; however, in the months following his mother's sudden death from what was surmised to be a drug overdose, Andy seemed to become increasingly preoccupied with sexual desire and arousal involving young adolescent males. Following that, Andy had sustained very discrete sexual encounters with six adolescents at the school. These encounters usually involved boys with the following profile: they came to him for "counseling," were from single-parent families, were loners, and had problems with low self-esteem.

Inevitability or Choice?

It may seem that the developmental trajectory of Rev. Sharff's life would most likely result in his ephebophilic behavior or that Rev. Gilliam would probably become a model of psychological and sexual integration. The reality is that predisposing factors as well as developmental factors do exert considerable influence on developmental outcomes, much as a sapling that is bent and secured in that position by a rope has a high probability of becoming a leaning tree. But the fact remains that, just as a bent sapling can be pulled back and secured in an upright position, so too can individuals refocus their developmental trajectory.

For instance, Jim Gilliam certainly appears to have had ideal parenting and many of the wholesome childhood and adolescent experiences that foster optimal development. Nevertheless, there were countless decision points in his life—on a daily basis—in which his practice of healthy and virtuous behaviors reinforced the growth-focused developmental path he continues to traverse. Despite his early developmental advantages, Jim could have made a series of everyday decisions that could have, over time, shifted his developmental trajectory in a less healthy direction. Similarly, despite Andy Sharff's high hormonal levels and molestation by an adult acquaintance, his eventual ephebophilic acting-out behavior was also influenced by a series of decisions on his part, and, quite possibly, on the part of his superiors. For example, he could have decided to decline the bishop's offer of a full-time ministry position that put him "in harm's way," or he could have decided to seek help with his compulsive masturbation. The fact that he did not, and that his superiors were either unaware or unconcerned about his sexual predilection, is telling. Granted, such choices require a certain degree of courage and resolve. Nevertheless, grace and the awareness and concern of others can and are often operative at such decision points. Thankfully, today there is growing awareness that the screening of candidates for ministry must include, in addition to a full psychological test battery, a detailed developmental history from pregnancy through the present, a spiritual history, work history, and criminal background check, and a thorough sexual history taken by someone with significant clinical experience in assessing the various factors and markers of psychosexual development. Had such a screening protocol been required when John Steffin and Andy Sharff were applying for seminary admission, a decision for nonacceptance might have been made.

Table 2-2 provides a capsule summary of the developmental factors that reflect the differing psychosexual trajectories in the lives of these three priests.

Table 2-2: Developmental Factors in the Lives of Three Priests

Developmental Factors	Rev. Jim Gilliam	Rev. John Steffin	Rev. Andy Sharff
parental attitude toward pregnancy; birth status re: complications	wanted; uneventful pregnancy and birth	ambivalence; uneventful pregnancy and birth	wanted but high risk pregnancy, birth complications
temperament; mother-infant "fit"	"easy"; good "fit"	"slow to warm"; poor "fit"	"difficult"; less than adequate "fit"
hormone levels, i.e., testosterone	normal	low	high
attachment style	secure	insecure-avoidant	insecure-ambivalent
early abuse history	none	emotional neglect	sexual molestation
family competence; family type or style	adequate to optimal; appropriate	midrange; enmeshed	midrange to borderline; disengaged
family attitudes re: sex and intimacy	positive; high commitment re: intimacy	negative; high commitment re: intimacy	permissive re: sex; low commitment re: intimacy
sexual self-exploration; self-soothing capacity	permitted; effective	punished; limited	permitted; somewhat ineffective
practice adult roles	"played house" taking father role	limited play-mates and opportunities	"played house" taking various roles
forge gender identity; parental identification	masculine; father	masculine; father	masculine? mother
have a best friend	yes	no	no
homosocial play; same-sex sexual exploration	yes; some	limited; none	yes; considerable
heterosexual parties; group dating	yes; yes	none; none	yes; some

Dev. Factors (cont.)	Rev. Gilliam (cont.)	Rev. Steffin (cont.)	Rev. Sharff (cont.)
onset/focus of sexual attraction feelings; onset of sexual fantasies	age 13, girls; age 14 same-age girls	none; none	age 12, primarily boys; age 13, same-age and younger boys
sexual expression; adolescent masturbation	occasional masturbation 14–17	very limited	regular to compulsive masturbation from 12 on
arousal pattern; sexual orientation	heterosexual	asexual	homosexual
skill re: physical and emotional intimacy	adequate to good	very poor	adequate
communicate effectively re: intimacy issues	adequate to good	very limited	limited to adequate
decision re: sexual lifestyle options	sexual celibacy, i.e., healthy friendships	avoid sexual and intimacy demands	focus on relations with adolescent males
balance self-interest with self-surrender; level of generativity	good balance, mature self-giving; high generativity	pseudo-self-surrender; low generativity	extreme self-preoccupation; low level of generativity
reaction to andropause (male menopause)	reaffirms celibacy	oblivious	upset at the prospect of losing youthful appearance

Concluding Note

This chapter began with examples of three apparently similar individuals whose lifelong psychosexual development took significantly different paths or trajectories. An integrative stage model of psychosexual development was then described. Thereafter, a detailed analysis of the three case histories illustrated the value of identifying predisposing and developmental factors which impact the process and outcomes of psychosexual development. The implication is that psychosexual development is a key component of a minister's overall human and spiritual development and that such an integrative model can be useful to formation personnel in both screening candidates for ministry and in guiding and advising them over the course of their formation.

References

Ainsworth, M., M. Blehar, E. Waters, and S. Walls. (1978). *Patterns of Attachment*. Hillsdale, N.J.: Erlbaum.

Beavers, R., and R. Hampson. (1990). *Successful Families: Assessment and Intervention*. New York: Norton.

Cavanagh, M. (1983). "The Impact of Psychosexual Growth on Marriage and Religious Life." *Human Development* 4 (3) 16–24.

Cozzens, D. (2000). *The Changing Face of the Priesthood*. Collegeville: Liturgical Press.

Crenshaw, T. (1996). *The Alchemy of Love and Lust*. New York: Putnam.

DeLamater, J., and W. Friedrich. (2002). "Human Sexual Development." *Journal of Sex Research* 39 (1) 10–14.

Karen, R. (1994). *Becoming Attached*. New York: Warner Books.

Longres, J. (2000). *Human Behavior in the Social Environment*. 3rd ed. Itasca, Ill.: Peacock.

Rossetti, S. (1990). *Slayer of the Soul: Child Sexual Abuse and the Catholic Church*. Mystic, Conn.: Twenty-Third Publications.

Siegel, D. (1999). *The Developing Mind*. New York: Guilford.

Sperry, L. (2001). "An Integrative Model of Pastoral Counseling and Spiritual Direction." *Human Development* 22 (2) 37–42.

Sperry, L. (2002). "From Psychopathology to Transformation: Retrieving the Developmental Focus in Psychotherapy." *Journal of Individual Psychology* 58:4.

Storms, M. (1981). "A Theory of Erotic Orientation Development." *Psychological Review* 88:340–53.

Thomas, A., and S. Chess. (1977). *Temperament and Development*. New York: Brunner/Mazel.

Whitehead E., and L. Whitehead. (1989). *A Sense of Sexuality: Christian Love and Intimacy*. New York: Doubleday.

Chapter 3

Sexuality, Intimacy, and Celibacy

Today, celibacy has become central in discussion about the sexual misconduct controversy. A sampling of talk show pundits and newspaper editorials suggests that, if celibacy were no longer required of priests, sexual improprieties would be virtually eliminated. That the media and the public, including many American Roman Catholics, consider priestly celibacy problematic suggests that they do not really understand the basic concept and value of celibacy. Needless to say, there is also considerable confusion about the relationship among sexual maturity, intimacy, and celibacy. And designations such as "sexual celibate," rather than clarify, seem to add to that confusion. Accordingly, a major challenge facing the Church today, and particularly those in ministry formation, is to better understand and articulate the relationship between sexuality and celibacy as well as that among sexuality, celibacy, and intimacy.

So what is intimacy and what is its connection to sexuality and celibacy? First, let's begin by defining intimacy. Ask any ten people to define intimacy and you will probably get ten different definitions. That is because intimacy is a lot like pornography. Most people know what it is when they experience it, but being able to clearly articulate its meaning is quite challenging. The same is true among researchers: there is still no consensus definition of intimacy. Despite this lack of consensus, intimacy researchers do "agree with the following premise: individuals have needs for both belonging and autonomy, and the

challenge of balancing these two needs is the basic challenge in intimate relationships" (Carlson and Sperry 1999:xx).

One measure of that capacity to effectively balance belonging and
dependency with autonomy or independence is reflected in the degree
to which an adult can respect others and their boundaries. Unfortunately, boundary violations are common in those who have problems
with intimacy and engage in sexual misconduct. Reflecting on their
many years of treating troubled clergy, Drs. Wayne Fehr and Don
Hands note that "clergy who manifest sexual misconduct or transgress boundaries generally are impoverished as far as intimacy with
self, others and God is concerned" (Fehr and Hands 1993:43).

This chapter highlights one of the book's basic premises: the integration of sexuality and intimacy is the endpoint of psychosexual development. Since the priesthood requires celibacy, this sexuality-intimacy
integration must necessarily include celibacy. Accordingly, the chapter
explores the relationship among sexuality, intimacy, and celibacy. It begins with discussing what intimacy is and what it is not. Next, it describes various types, levels, styles, and barriers to intimacy. Then it
turns to the topic of celibacy and the developmental stages of celibacy,
the meaning of celibate intimacy, and the relation of celibacy to intimacy, sexuality, and spirituality.

A Context for Thinking about Intimacy

To answer the question about the meaning of intimacy it is useful
to have a context for conceptualization of this complex, multifaceted
phenomenon. Before proceeding, it must be clear what intimacy is
and what it is not. We begin by saying what it is not.

What Intimacy Is and Is Not. Intimacy is not sex, love, passion
or certain kinds of relationships. First of all, intimacy is not sex or
sexual activity. Neither is intimacy the same as love, although love is
an element of intimacy. Neither is intimacy the same as passion—an
intense emotional state of various and sometimes confusing feelings.
Neither is intimacy a collegial relationship; nor is it a casual or fair-
weather friendship.

On the other hand, intimacy is a special kind of relationship that reflects a fundamental survival need for attachment. Attachment is the
emotional bond that develops between infant and mother or caregiver
(Karen 1994). Disruptions or failures in the mother-infant attachment
bond have dire consequences in the short run and the long run. In the

short run, infants without some human connectedness fail to thrive and eventually die. In the long run, severe disruption of this attachment bond has dire consequences for the development of true intimacy later in life. Such consequences include sexual and marital problems, divorce, and various psychiatric and substance disorders. This need for intimacy is developmentally "a more mature, differentiated and advanced manifestation of the universal biological need for physical closeness, connection, and contact with another human being" (Bagarozzi 2002:7).

A very basic definition of intimacy is that it involves both promoting closeness or bondedness *and* the experience of warmth or affection in a human relationship. The sense of closeness can include emotional, intellectual, social, and spiritual bonds. However, not all close relationships would be considered intimate. For example, while you may work closely with a colleague, the relationship would not be considered intimate unless the second component, i.e., the experience of warmth and personal sharing, is present.

Mature vs. Immature Intimacy. Intimacy can be further conceptualized as mature and immature. While there may be a close, warm mother-infant bond, the bond would be considered immature since there can be no equal sharing of power or respect for each other's boundaries, since the infant has not yet developed those capacities. Needless to say, adults without these capacities can only experience immature intimacy. On the other hand, mature intimate relationships involve both a sharing of power as well as mutual respect for the other's personal boundaries. Furthermore, mature intimacy can be thought of as a close, familiar, and often affectionate personal relationship with another person that involves an in-depth knowledge of the person as well as a reciprocal expression of one's thoughts, feelings, and sentiments. Such closeness in friendships or in romantic relationships inevitably entail ambivalent feeling, both positive and negative, which can coexist. Accordingly, mature intimacy involves learning to live with this ambivalence, both the exhilaration and the strain that comes with being close.

Pseudo-Intimacy. It is important to differentiate mature intimacy from pseudo-intimacy, which is a form of immature intimacy. Pseudo-intimacy is a relationship that appears to involve intimacy but does not. In pseudo-intimacy an intense sexual feeling typically substitutes for genuine intimacy and the true nature of a relationship is kept secret in order to maintain a fiction and to avoid confrontation. Pseudo-intimacy is a game of pretense which "allows both parties to pretend that what is happening is not really happening" (Lothstein

1990:39). At its best, only a partial relationship is formed. For example, an adult may establish a relationship with another adult who cannot share deeply or be emotionally available because that person is already involved in committed relationship or is a workaholic and utilizes work and busyness to avoid the risks of relating. Or, an adult may believe that he or she has formed a close, deep intimate relationship with a child, when, in fact, the child is not developmentally ready to share power in a relationship that is one requisite of mature intimacy. Such relationships are psychologically safe for the adult because one does not need to risk a total sharing of one's self, particularly one's deepest hopes and fears. On the other hand, when such a relationship involves sexual abuse great harm can result.

Pseudo-intimacy is not uncommon in ministry today particularly because of the prevalence of both dependency and narcissism in priests and other ministers. Individuals with significant dependent and narcissistic features are capable of little more than pseudo-intimacy. For the narcissistic individual, intimacy means nothing more than being admired or adored and basking in the glow of another. For the dependent individual, intimacy means relating to another person who will take over responsibility and provide approval for his or her immature behavior (Masterson 2000).

Sex and Intimacy. What is the place of sex in intimacy? Sex may or may not play a role in intimate relationships, just as intimacy may or may not accompany sexual activity. The expression of sexuality in intimacy can range from gentle touch to genital intercourse. The next section further amplifies sexual intimacy as well as other types of intimacy.

Types of Intimacy

For many, intimacy typically connotes physical or sexual intimacy. In actuality, intimacy comes in a variety of flavors or types. This section briefly describes and differentiates several types of intimacy. These distinctions are essential background for a informed discussion of the relationship of intimacy, sexuality, and celibacy.

Sexual intimacy refers to the sexuality in an intimate relationship in all its variations, ranging from gentle touch to genital intercourse. It is eroticized intimacy and thus can be distinguished from noneroticized or physical or nonsexual intimacy. Nonsexual intimacy refers to various types of intimacy without genital expression. These include emotional intimacy, intellectual intimacy, social intimacy, psychological intimacy, and spiritual intimacy. Table 3-1 provides a capsule description of these seven types of intimacy along with celibate intimacy.

Table 3-1: Eight Types of Intimacy*

Type of Intimacy	Description
Sexual Intimacy	communicating, sharing, and expressing feelings, thoughts, fantasies, and desires of a sexual nature with a significant other. It includes physical closeness, contact and interactions intended to be sexually arousing, stimulating, and satisfying; but it may or may not lead to sexual intercourse and/or orgasm for one or both parties.
Physical (Nonsexual) Intimacy	engaging in physical closeness and body contact with a significant other, i.e., hugging, giving a back rub or other nonsexual touching, that is not a prelude to genital sexual activity.
Psychological Intimacy	communicating, sharing and disclosing personal information and feelings about oneself with a significant other. other. It may include disclosing one's hopes and dreams as well as one's fears, concerns, and insecurities. True psychological intimacy presumes a secure base of trust in the relationship.
Intellectual Intimacy	communicating and sharing important ideas, thoughts, beliefs, etc., with a significant other. It presumes the capacity for role-taking, i.e., to understand the world from the other's frame of reference.
Emotional Intimacy	communicating and sharing all of one's feelings, both positive and negative, with a significant other. It presumes empathy, i.e., the capacity for putting one's self in another's place *and* feeling what the other is feeling without identifying with or feeling sorry for the other, i.e., sympathy.
Social Intimacy	engaging in enjoyable or playful activities and experiences with a significant other. Can include sharing one's daily experiences, discussing current events, or sharing meals, etc.
Spiritual Intimacy	sharing one's thoughts, feelings, beliefs, and experiences about spiritual matters or concerns with a significant other, as well as God. May include religious practices, rituals, experiences of nature or deep personal spiritual experiences.
Celibate Intimacy	sharing a deep friendship without being married and without violating chastity physically or psychologically. For a priest, this form of intimacy is considered by some to be a gift and a grace.

*informed in part by Bagarozzi (2001)

Levels and Styles of Intimacy

Besides specifying types of intimacy it is useful and necessary to further describe the depth or level of intimacy as well as the particular and favored patterns or styles of intimacy manifested in committed relationships. This section describes various levels and styles of intimacy.

Levels of Intimacy

Both clinical observation and research suggest that intimacy is not a skill that most individuals and couples exhibit or possess the capacity to consistently experience it. This is not to suggest that intimacy is an all-or-nothing phenomenon wherein certain individuals can rather consistently experience it, while other individuals never experience it. There is also a group of individuals who are capable of occasionally experiencing it such as in times of crisis such as funerals or following a serious accident. Rather, it appears that there are discrete levels of relational functioning that have been noted in individuals and couples. It is postulated that intimacy can only be sustained at higher levels of relational functioning. Following are descriptions of three different conceptualizations of levels of relational functioning.

The Spiral Model of Intimacy: L'Abate (1986; 1997) has proposed a developmental model of interpersonal competence which highlights intimacy and its determinants. He defines intimacy as the sharing of joys, hurts, and fears of being hurt. Research indicates that such sharing leads to committed, close, and prolonged relationships, while inability to engage in such sharing results in relational dysfunction.

Three prerequisites for intimacy are equality, commitment, and reciprocity or mutuality in the relationship. From these flow six processes that produce what L'Abate (1997) calls the "spiral of intimacy": communication of personal values, respect for personal feelings, acceptance of personal limitations, affirmation, sharing of hurts and fears of being hurt, and forgiveness of errors. The sharing of hurts represents the ability to be independent or separate and dependent or together simultaneously. It requires the strength to join another in sharing hurt, while being separate enough to be available to the other without the demand for perfection, solutions, or performance. L'Abate also notes that crying together is the ultimate demonstration of sharing hurts. Unconditional love is demonstrated by the ability to be available, which is defined as the ability to be available to share hurts

or cry together. Consequently, individuals who do not possess sufficient resources to share hurts can only love conditionally, resulting in
limited intimacy.

In other words, there are two levels of intimacy: "intimacy" and
"non-intimacy." The intimacy level includes six progressively related
sublevels: communication → respect → acceptance → affirmation →
sharing of hurts → forgiveness. Note that, just as sharing of hurts requires four requisite skills or sublevels, true forgiveness requires all
five requisites. The non-intimacy level is notably deficient in one or
more of these sublevels.

Levels of Relational Stability: Based on extensive research,
Gottman (1993; 1994a; 1994b) describes intimacy in terms of levels
of relational stability. While this research was primarily based on
committed couples, the findings are applicable to committed friendship relationships as well. The key finding is that lasting and satisfying intimate relationships depend on both individuals' capacity to
reasonably cope with conflicts that are inevitable in a relationship.
Gottman has described two levels of relational stability: stable and
unstable. Stable relationships involve relational styles marked by efforts to cope with occasional conflict and the capacity to maintain intimacy. Such behaviors are predictive of relational satisfaction, personal
growth, and the continuance of the relationship.

On the other hand, unstable relationships involve relational styles
marked by ongoing conflict and the inability to maintain intimacy.
Not surprisingly, such behaviors are predictive of increased dissatisfaction and noncontinuance of the relationship. By definition, individuals in stable relationships are more likely to exhibit and experience
intimacy than individuals in unstable relationships.

Styles of Intimacy

A corollary to Gottman's research on levels of relational stability
is research on differing styles of intimacy. Gottman conceptualized
intimacy styles in terms of stylistic ways or patterns in which individuals engaged in conflict resolution or problem solving in their relationships. Five different styles of conflict resolution were observed:
Validating, Volatile, Conflict-Avoiding, Hostile, and Hostile-Detached.
The first three of these styles were noted in stable relationships, while
the last two stylistic patterns were observed primarily in unstable relationships. Table 3-2 describes these five styles of intimacy with regard to two levels of relational stability.

Gottman (1994b) observes a culture bias in America regarding the validating style. Since the validating style is more compatible with a romantic view of life as well as a client-centered view of psychotherapy, many assume that this style is the ideal for which all relationships should strive and the unspoken criterion on which relationships are judged. Specifically, the media and therapists idealize relationships in which individuals can compromise, work out problems calmly, and accept the other's unique differences. Despite the fact that research indicates that the volatile and conflict-avoiding styles are also stable and satisfying ways of relating intimately, these relational patterns tend to be viewed as less than ideal. Needless to say, the implications of this bias—not only for relationships but also for clinical practice, therapist training, and research—are immense.

Finally, Gottman views couples' relationships from a behavioral exchange–balance theory perspective. He has operationalized effective relational functioning of the couple system in terms of the ratio of positive feelings and interactions to negative feelings and interactions. Using a variety of measures—laughter, touching, facial expression, physiological measures, and frequency of fights—Gottman found that a ratio of five or more positive interactions to one negative predicts relational stability, while a lesser ratio predicts relational dissolution. In fact, this ratio can predict relational success with 94 percent accuracy.

Gottman (1994a) has also identified four warning signs that the relationship is failing. They are: criticism, contempt, defensiveness, and stonewalling. *Criticism, i.e., ad hominem,* involves personalizing, blaming, and character attacking. *Contempt* involves devaluation as well as the desire to hurt, demean, or insult the other. As a result, feelings of closeness and the capacity to compliment and support the other are lost in a flurry of sneering, eye-rolling, and name-calling. *Defensiveness* involves feeling hurt, victimized, and responding to deflect blows by making excuses and refusing any responsibility for change. Finally, *stonewalling* involves emotionally withdrawing from the other in the face of conflict or demands in an attempt to decrease the conflict. Unfortunately, in the long run, this strategy actually increases relational distress and disharmony. While these four negative affects are prominent in unstable relationships, they can occasionally be seen in stable relationships as well.

Table 3-2: Levels and Styles of Intimacy (Based on Gottman 1994b)

Level/Style	Description
Stable	relational styles marked by efforts to cope with occasional conflict and the capacity to maintain intimacy
Validating	characterized by their capacity to compromise, to work out problems calmly, and to accept their partner's unique differences
Volatile	characterized by occasional intense disputes, and may be defensive and act critically toward one another. Nevertheless, they seem to enjoy their intensity, which is followed by a renewed sense of commitment and an increased sense of individuality.
Conflict-Avoiding	characterized by avoiding disagreements, minimizing them or engaging in solitary activities to handle or relieve tensions. Despite their distancing of conflict, these relationships are relatively happy and satisfying.
Unstable	relational styles marked by ongoing conflict and the inability to maintain intimacy
Hostile	characterized by intense disputes that involve criticism, contempt and defensiveness. These disputes are neither followed by a renewal of the relationship nor an increased sense of individuality but rather to eventual dissolution.
Hostile-Detached	characterized by a pattern of intense disputes that involves an increasing criticalness and contempt in one individual that predictably prompts an emotional withdrawal by the other. This pattern fosters defensiveness in both individuals and eventually increases the probability of dissolution.

Barriers to Intimacy

Barriers to intimacy refer to specific behaviors, skill deficits, or dispositions that effectively block or prevent an individual from forming or maintaining a close bond with another. These include failure to distinguish sex from intimacy, lack of trust, lack of empathy, a sense of specialness and self-entitlement, poor boundaries and fear of engulfment, homophobia, lack of self-esteem, and impaired communication (McClone 2002; Kenel 2002). In and of itself, the presence of a character or personality disorder, such as the narcissistic or anti-social personality disorder, is also a major barrier to intimacy. Table 3-3 describes eight such barriers.

Table 3-3: Barriers to Intimacy

Barrier	Description
Failure to Distinguish Sex from Intimacy	equating sexual activity with intimacy can result in a limited capacity for developing and maintaining healthy interpersonal relationships
Lack of Trust	lacking the capacity to believe in the honesty and integrity of others limits one's willingness to expect another to keep confidences and not betray or undermine one's efforts in and outside interpersonal relationships
Lack of Empathy	lacking the capacity for thinking and feeling what another is thinking and feeling interferes with the development of emotional intimacy
A Sense of Specialness and Self-Entitlement	narcissistic traits such as specialness and entitlement, i.e., the unreasonable expectation of having all one's needs met and given favorable treatment, and a lack of empathy are incompatible with relationships based on equality and reciprocity
Poor Boundaries and/or a Fear of Engulfment	the fear that one will be psychologically engulfed by another because of poor boundaries, difficulties setting limits, or problems managing one's own sexual arousal, anxiety, or anger
Homophobia	an irrational fear of or bias against homosexuality or homosexual individuals in a male which can lead to difficulty in establishing close friendship relationships with other men
Lack of Self-Esteem	the inability to view and accept oneself as worthwhile and loveable delimits the likelihood of communicating an attitude of self-acceptance, self-approval, and self-respect to others
Impaired Communication	a limited capacity to listen actively and to respond appropriately with empathy and assertiveness seriously impairs the development and maintenance of intimate relationships

Celibacy

Priestly celibacy is a way of life characterized by continence or renunciation of marriage for the sake of the reign of God. Related to celibacy is chastity, "the virtue by which human sexuality is ordered to its proper purpose. . . . More than continence, it is the virtue that pursues the integration of the true meaning of sexuality and intimacy, whether one is married or not" (McBrien 1995:302–03). Unfortunately, these concepts appear to be little understood or respected by some—including the media—who insist that clergy sexual misconduct is attributable to celibacy.

Celibacy can be likened to a journey that is conditioned by personality factors, institutional expectations, and the immediate context that impact individuals. Bonnot (1995) offers an astute observation. He contends that every person who commits to a celibate life experiences several different celibacies. He means that as a person matures he or she negotiates various developmental stages of celibacy.

Stages of Celibacy

These are based, in part, on Erikson's stage theory of psychosocial development. Like stage theories, Bonnot (1995) proposes a stage model in which each stage has a distinctive challenge that is prominent at one time and recessive at other times but nevertheless impacts an individual. Each stage demands and requires the resolution of a specific challenge or dilemma, and requires specific strengths, for its resolution carries through into subsequent stages with varying degrees of influence. More specifically, each stage of celibacy demands and requires the resolution of a specific challenge or dilemma and requires specific strengths for its resolution and cultivates specific virtues. These virtues "enable the challenge of celibacy to be lived thereafter with success and satisfaction" (p. 19).

Table 3-4 characterizes these four developmental stages.

Intimacy, Sexuality, Celibacy, and Spirituality

This section discusses and clarifies the relationship between intimacy and celibacy. Both intimacy and celibacy are closely related developmental lines of psychosexual development. Accordingly, the developmental endpoint of psychosexual development and emotional maturity can be conceptualized as integration, unity, or union. In *The*

Changing Face of the Priesthood, Donald Cozzens describes intimacy as the innate longing or desire for union with another.

Table 3-4: Developmental Stages of Celibacy*

Stages	Description
Adolescent	This stage extends from puberty into the late twenties and can be thought of as the stage of physical celibacy. *Physical celibacy* refers to the capacity to be fully human without either being sexually active or frustrated and distracted. Resolution of this stage presumes one has forged a vision of celibacy as a worthwhile lifestyle choice. This stage approximates Erikson's stage of identity.
Generative	This stage extends from the late twenties into the middle thirties and can be called generative celibacy. *Generative celibacy* refers to the capacity to be productive and responsible without becoming a parent nor feeling deprived and incomplete. Resolution of this stage requires assuming responsibility for the community as a whole, for the life and well-being of the next generation. This stage approximates Erikson's stage of generativity.
Intimate	This stage extends from the mid-thirties to the late fifties and is called intimate celibacy. *Intimate celibacy* refers to the capacity to be a life-sharing friend without being married, as well as not violating chastity physically or psychologically. This is the most challenging stage of intimacy and one of the most difficult to accomplish within current structures of the Church. Resolution of this stage presumes acceptance of the intimacy of companionship as enhancing one's life and ministry. This stage approximates Erikson's stage of intimacy.
Integral	This stage extends from the late fifties to retirement and death and can be thought of as integral celibacy. *Integral celibacy* refers to the capacity to maintain meaning and hope about one's contributions to life in the face of retirement and declining health and to find reasons to carry on as one's friends and peers retire or die. Resolution of this stage presumes acceptance of the decisions and experiences of one's past life without despair or regret. This stage approximates Erikson's stage of wisdom.

*based on Bonnot 1995

Celibate Intimacy. Celibate intimacy is the capacity to share a deep friendship without being married and without violating chastity physically or psychologically. Developmentally, it is the third of the four stages of celibacy (Bonnot 1995). For a priest this form of intimacy is considered to be a gift and a grace and is most likely to be realized in emotionally mature priests (Cozzens 2000).

As previously noted, emotional maturity requires a high degree of psychosexual development. Such maturity is the foundation for authentic spirituality and inevitably involves the capacity to initiate and maintain healthy relationships. Without such maturity, priests are likely to be underdeveloped spiritually and intellectually and experience increasing longing and emptiness in their lives. Many priests attempt to relieve this emptiness, a reflection of the basic desire for union, with possession, prestige, or power. Unfortunately, such relief is only temporary and the inherent longing for union only increases. Without a few really close and intimate friends the priest's hunger for romantic or sexual relationships may become overwhelming (Cozzens 2000).

Unmet intimacy needs "have led countless priests to think they could find true fulfillment only in marriage or, in the case of the homosexually oriented priest, in a sexually active relationship with another man. Whatever the orientation, the priest gives serious thought to leaving the priesthood in order to meet his soul's desire for union" (Cozzens 2000:31). He adds: "The real question is not whether to leave and marry, rather it is to discern if he and his beloved can commit to a celibate friendship. In other words, is he experiencing a vocational crisis or an intimacy crisis? . . . crises of intimacy sometimes lead to exploitative relationships with a number of women or men" (p. 32).

Sexual Celibacy. A somewhat similar formulation of celibate intimacy has been described by Donald Goergen (1974) in *The Sexual Celibate* as sexual celibacy. Sexual celibacy is an expression of sexuality that is centered on friendship and which strives after nongenital intimacy. Goergen explores the terrain of intimacy and celibacy along the continuum from genital to nongenital intimacy. Not surprisingly, he considers the implications of genital sexual activity, particularly masturbation, in the development process of celibacy.

Masturbation involves self-stimulation of the genitals to achieve erotic gratification. Traditionally, masturbation was always considered self-abuse and thus harmful and sinful. Today, when viewed from a developmental perspective, a more differentiated understanding emerges. In this perspective infantile and adolescent masturbation is viewed more as exploratory behavior, while occasional masturbation in adulthood may serve as an outlet for tension. Nevertheless, abusive or compulsive forms tend to be viewed as harmful or sinful. With regard to masturbation and celibacy, Goergen insists that while "masturbation is not a sign of perfection we as celibates strive to live, neither is it sin. It is simply imperfection—that which we all are and yet strive to overcome. . . . Masturbation points to unfinishedness of the process of spiritualization."

Sexuality, Celibacy, and Spirituality. Sexuality can also be viewed in relation to spirituality. Among the many ways of describing Christian spirituality is a patterning of life around the experience of God in a faith community centered in Christ and the embracing of the life of the flesh. Furthermore, being created in the image of God to seek and enjoy union is a basic human striving reflected in our psychological development from birth (Friberg and Laaser 1998). Since psychological development inevitably includes sexual development, spirituality and sexuality are integrally related. Finally, spirituality can also be related to intimacy, such that spiritual intimacy is described as a sense of closeness and bonding with God.

Concluding Note

Just as sexual development proceeds through stages from less mature and integrated to more mature and integrated, so does intimacy and celibacy. Different views of the development or levels of intimacy were described as were the various types, styles, and barriers to intimacy. Similarly, the stages of the development of celibacy were described. This developmental perspective on intimacy and celibacy was a prelude to a discussion of the relationship among sexuality, intimacy, and celibacy, as well as spirituality.

References

Bagarozzi, D. (2001). *Enhancing Intimacy in Marriage: A Clinician's Guide*. New York: Brunner/Routeledge.

Bonnot, B. (1995). "Stages in a Celibate's Life." *Human Development* 16 (3) 18–22.

Carlson, J., and L. Sperry. (1999). "Preface." In J. Carlson, and L. Sperry, eds., *The Intimate Couple*. New York: Brunner/Mazel. xix–xxi.

Cozzens, D. (2000). *The Changing Face of the Priesthood*. Collegeville: Liturgical Press.

Fehr, W., and D. Hands. (1993). *Spiritual Wholeness for Clergy*. Washington, D.C.: Alban Institute.

Friberg, N., and M. Laaser. (1998). *Before the Fall: Preventing Pastoral Sexual Abuse*. Collegeville: Liturgical Press.

Goergen, D. (1974). *The Sexual Celibate*. New York: Seabury.

Gottman, J. (1993). "The Roles of Conflict Engagement, Escalation, and Avoidance in Marital Interaction: A Longitudinal View of Five Types of Couples." *Journal of Consulting and Clinical Psychology* 61 (1) 6–15.

Gottman, J. (1994a). "An Agenda for Marital Therapy." In S. Johnson, and L. Greenberg, eds., *The Heart of the Matter: Perspectives on Emotion in Marital Therapy*. New York: Brunner/Mazel. 256–93.

Gottman, J. (1994b). *Why Marriages Succeed or Fail*. New York: Simon & Schuster.

Karen, R. (1994). *Becoming Attached*. New York: Warner Books.

Kenel, M. (2002). "Impediments to Intimacy." *Human Development* 23 (1) 29–35.

L'Abate, L. (1986). *Systematic Family Therapy*. New York: Brunner/Mazel.

L'Abate, L. (1997). *The Self in the Family: A Classification of Personality, Criminality and Psychopathology*. New York: Wiley.

Lothstein, L. (1990). "Psychological Theories of Pedophilia and Ephebophilia." In S. Rossetti, ed., *Slayer of the Soul: Child Sexual Abuse and the Catholic Church*. Collegeville: Liturgical Press. 9–44.

Masterson, J. (2000). *The Personality Disorders: A New Look at the Developmental Self and Object Relations Approach*. Phoenix, Ariz.: Zeig, Tucker.

McBrien, R. (1995). *The Harpercollins Encyclopedia of Catholicism*. San Francisco: HarperSanFrancisco.

McClone, K. (2002). "Male Intimacy." *Human Development* 23 (1) 5–11.

Chapter 4

Determinants of Ministry Health and Sexual Misconduct

Curt Conway was forty-four years old when his world started to cave in. Basically, Curt was a well-liked, hardworking priest who would never refuse a request to help anyone in need. It was during the third year of an assignment to a very needy central-city parish that Curt began experiencing anxiety attacks that compounded his chronic insomnia. For twenty-six years Curt had belonged to a religious congregation noted for its undaunted commitment to the poor. At first, Curt's personal physician had prescribed Valium for his symptoms. Initially, the medication had worked, but ever-increasing doses were needed to calm Curt's furies. It was then that he stopped taking the medication and sought psychological counseling that focused on coping and stress management. Like the medication, this seem to help for a while, but nine months later Curt's superior arranged for him to take a sabbatical leave when his depressive symptoms worsened.

Curt was assigned to a renewal center, where he participated in a comprehensive treatment program that included psychiatric and preventive care as well as spiritual renewal. During the course of the program, he was able to step back and assess his own psychosexual and spirituality health, the patterns of stresses in his recent pastoral assignments, his theology of ministry, and the structure and culture of his religious order, as well as his own health and personality in terms of strengths and vulnerabilities. He was shocked at the treatment team's assessment and recommendations. They noted that Curt presented an asexual orientation, had no real close friends, and little experience of emotional intimacy. It appeared that his depression was based as much in this emotionally isolative realm as it was in being burnt-out. In consultation with his superior, and as part of his aftercare, Curt was assigned to the formation team at the order's scholasticate. There the setting, structure, and culture of his ministry would be more reflective and less driven.

As part of its corporate strategic planning, the order had decided that the increasing numbers of priests who were burning out and becoming impaired called for a reexamination of the order's style of ministry. They concluded that change was indeed necessary, beginning with formation. During his sabbatical, Curt had taken some graduate courses in spirituality and supervised experience in spiritual direction that prepared him to assume some spiritual direction responsibilities in the order's formation house. He continued in his aftercare for two years, during which time he adapted with some difficulty to a new style and mode of ministry and living. Four years later, Curt continued to live a relatively balanced and rewarding lifestyle.

Curt's case exemplifies a number of features common in professional ministries today: high-demand ministry, impaired psychosexual development, limited capacity for emotional intimacy, the burnout-prone culture of a diocese or religious order, and ministry reentry and reassignment. But it also points up a number of questions, including: Why were psychological counseling and stress management ineffective? Was there any relationship between Curt's asexual orientation and his religious order's culture? Would Curt's recovery have come about if changes in his theology of ministry and the order's organizational structure and culture, as well as reassignment, had not occurred? A basic understanding that many have of stress and burnout is that they represent deficits in an individual's ability to cope with stress, rather than deficits in that person's job or the organization of which he or she is a part. Therefore, it should not be surprising that stress-management programs focus on improving employees' or managers' ability to accommodate and to cope with the stresses of the job and the organization. It has been our observation that burnout and impairment are as much a function of organizational structure, culture, and the individual's beliefs about his or her professional functioning, i.e., their theology of ministry, as they are a function of stresses of the job or of individual vulnerabilities and lack of coping skills.

This chapter describes four interactive factors or determinants that, taken together, are suggestive of whether a minister or priest is more likely to experience ministry health, on the one hand, or impairment, particularly sexual misconduct, on the other hand. Each of these determinants will be described and illustrated in the following sections.

Four Determinants

On the basis of organizational systems theory and my experience as a consultant to religious organizations, there appear to be four intersecting determinants involved in ministerial sexual misconduct. The four are: minister, institution or organizational dynamics, ministry assignment, and relationships. These determinants are derived from a formula for understanding ministry health and impairment described several years ago (Sperry 1991). These four determinants represent several internal and external factors influencing health and impairment. When there is a good "fit" or synchrony among these four, the minister will experience a high degree of well-being and wholeness. Conversely, when there is a poor "fit" among two or more of these, the minister is likely to experience some degree of distress or even impairment. Impairment can take several forms including physical conditions, psychiatric conditions (cf. Sperry 2000) or sexual misconduct. This formula of four determinants provides a useful framework for understanding and predicting, in general terms, the likelihood of a priest's health and well-being or of sexual misconduct in ministry. Figure 4-1 illustrates this formula.

Figure 4-1: Determinants of Ministry Health and Misconduct

Minister (+) Organizational Dynamics (+) Assignment (+) Relational Dynamics → Health or Misconduct

This chapter will describe each of these four determinants of ministry health or impairment, particularly, sexual misconduct. Subsequent chapters, particularly those in Part II, further elaborate aspects of this formula.

Minister

The first dimension, the minister as individual, includes several internal factors that influence a minister's overall health and well-being.

These include various strengths and vulnerabilities. Of particular interest are level of psychosexual and spiritual development, and various personality and character features such as degree of entitlement, abusiveness, and compulsivity, as well as one's theology of ministry.

With regard to psychosexual development, chapter 2 has described the various determinants of level of psychosexual—and spiritual—development, while chapter 8 describes ways of assessing it. Chapters 5 and 7 describe the role of abusiveness and compulsivity in sexual misconduct, while chapter 6 describes how narcissistic entitlement influences sexual behavior. Theology of ministry is described here.

Theology of Ministry. How an individual views his or her professional role and responsibilities can greatly influence that person's job performance, level of stress, and general sense of personal well-being. For example, the physician who believes that he or she must cure patients and defy death at all costs will approach patients and respond to stress differently from the physician who believes that his or her basic role is to encourage patients to take responsibility for their health.

A minister's theology of ministry will greatly influence the purpose of, and the approach to, his or her ministry. Basically, then, there are two widely differing theologies of ministry. In one, the call to ministry is heard as a personal responsibility in which the minister focuses talented energy on serving others, upholding established policy and authority, maintaining hierarchy and control, and preserving the status quo. In this view, the health and well-being of the minister is a secondary consideration in the accomplishment of the mission. The focus is on action and results and the "doing" pole of existence. On the other hand, the call to ministry can be heard as a commitment to model the Lord's wholeness through presence, discernment, mutuality, empowerment, and transformation. In this view, the minister's own balanced lifestyle and mutual concern become the media through which the kingdom comes about. Doing springs from the "being" pole of existence, as action flows from contemplation. It is my clinical observation that a balanced and healthy theology of ministry is one that keeps the individual in touch with his or her humanity.

Since American culture emphasizes "doing over being" and doing things right, it shouldn't be surprising that many ministers are perfectionists and espouse a similar theology of ministry. Generally speaking, perfectionists share a belief in the three Os: omnipotence, omniscience, and omnipresence. They act as though they must take responsibility for everything, and they find it difficult to delegate decision-making to others (omnipotence). They believe that they should be totally competent and know everything there is to know about their work (omniscience). Finally, they believe that they should be available to those they serve seven days a week, twenty-four hours a day, which effectively precludes time for rest and recreation (omnipresence). The three Os suggest godlike strivings that require Herculean energy and commitment that few can maintain for long. Not surprisingly, anxiety, depression, guilt, self-doubt, and chronic frustration are common psychological symptoms experienced by these individuals. Chapter 7 describes various types of priests involved in sexual misconduct, including some whose theology of ministry has an operative influence in their sexual problems.

Curt admitted that his spiritual life was unbalanced, with little or no time for prayer amid his many responsibilities. During the course of his treatment, Curt was helped to articulate his beliefs and assumptions about ministry. His theology of ministry was characterized by such beliefs as "Service to others is its own reward"; "I am called to be a person for others"; "The need of the community comes before my personal needs"; and "I am called to be perfect." These beliefs probably accurately reflect not only his novitiate and seminary training but also his theological assumptions and ministry style. These other-oriented beliefs will also show up as resistance to psychotherapy and health care when the focus involves self-care and personal well-being. Often, an individual such as Curt will initially view the need for nurturance and self-care as contradictory to his or her religious training.

Organizational Dynamics

Organizational dynamics include structural and cultural aspects of the religious organization, i.e., religious order or diocese, that can significantly affect a minister's health or impairment. Organizational factors can significantly impact the attitudes and behaviors of members of the organizations. In fact, organizational factors can exert considerably more influence over an individual than one's personality and values. Because Americans are enamored of self-determination, they tend to downplay the influence of organizational dynamics on their lives. Nevertheless, there are far too many examples of the overpowering influence of such organizational factors.

A case in point is the Los Angeles Police Department (LAPD) in the 1980s. After Daryl Gates became police chief, LAPD quickly got the reputation for having more formal complaints of physical, verbal, emotional, and sexual abusiveness filed by employees than any other organization or corporation in the state of California. While the public was aware of police brutality in the community—due largely to the Rodney King incident—few knew of the extent of the abusiveness and brutality that occurred within the LAPD, among officers and other employees. Since prior to Gates' tenure as police chief there were relatively few complaints of abusiveness, organizational researchers analyzed the structure and culture that developed under Gates' leadership. They found that the structure and culture fostered, and even rewarded, abusiveness by police officers toward citizens of Los Angeles and within the department itself. A similar phenomenon has been noted in seminaries and male religious orders that shifted from a respectful attitude toward women to one of misogyny, hatred and disrespect of women, as a new administration came into leadership. Often, such major shifts are observable within six to twelve months.

Curt belongs to a medium-sized, progressive religious congregation whose mission includes high-school, college, and seminary teaching as well as parish work. Most of the members of Curt's province were involved in central-city ministry work and were deeply committed to justice and peace issues, while those involved in teaching were less so. Not surprisingly, this accounted for considerable tension within the order, particularly in Curt's province. The provincial leadership had recently changed, and although there was some hope that morale would increase, immediate priorities involved both financial and personnel matters. Benevolent but autocratic leadership with high expectations for achievement had characterized the management of the province as far back as Curt could recall, and strategic planning had never been a priority. Decisions about personnel assignments and policy matters seemed to have been based more on arbitrary decisions than on long-range planning or needs assessment of individuals or institutions. Although Curt was not usually one to complain and had difficulty showing his anger, he was able to get in touch with some of the anger and ambiguity he felt about the arbitrariness and lack of trust and approachability of his superiors and his deep sadness and loneliness over the years as he struggled to be affirmed by his superiors as a "good" religious.

Organizational Design. Soroka (1986) suggests that the organizational design of the Church itself may be the primary source and cause of stress experienced by ministers. He notes that organizational design refers to the formal, rational properties of an organization that can be readily controlled by those responsible for designing and/or managing it, such as the bishop of a diocese or a major superior. Components of organizational design that are particularly important in a discussion of ministry, health, and impairment are role structure, power structure, and the normative structure and culture of the organization.

Role Structure. Role structure refers to the ways in which tasks and duties are stated, organized, and allocated among specific roles in a setting. Person-role conflict becomes evident in situations in which the minister's ideals come in conflict with organizational self-interest and the Church's bureaucratic mode of functioning. Role ambiguity occurs when the minister lacks information necessary to perform his role. Some sources of role ambiguity may be inherent in the minister's role, such as the lack of clear feedback concerning the results of one's work among others. In short, role structure affects the job-related stress of ministers through its impact on role conflict and ambiguity. Role conflict and ambiguity make it difficult for ministers to meet the demands associated with their vocation. Consequently, ministers may find it difficult or impossible to achieve a sense of psychological and personal well-being in their work.

Power Structure. Another aspect of organizational design is the power structure. The degree to which a minister is able to exercise power and control over his work setting will influence the extent to which he feels helpless. Research shows convincingly that individuals with high job demands and little or no decisional control over their work situation tend to experience serious medical conditions, such as heart attacks, strokes, and cancer, and psychiatric conditions, such as clinical depression, more than individuals with high job demands but more actual or perceived decisional control over their work situations (Karasek and Theorell 1990). The Church's centralized and hierarchical approach to decision-making effectively limits the autonomy and decisional control ministers experience in their work, contributing to their sense of helplessness, stress, and health problems.

Normative Structure. The normative structure of the Church consists of its goals, norms, beliefs, and culture. The Church's normative structure typically has not rewarded innovation, creativity, and risk-taking. Rather, it has emphasized its mission of service to others in the organization, with minimal encouragement of personal growth or the pursuit of knowledge as legitimate goals and activities in themselves. Accordingly, individuals who advocate innovation are not perceived as loyal and hardworking organization people. In short, role, power, and normative structures significantly influence and impact priests and their personal and ministerial life.

Culture. Culture refers to the shared values, attitudes, beliefs, stories, memories, rituals and actions that characterize an organization. It also includes the norms, the organization's unwritten "policies" about what is and what is not acceptable. Culture is to the organization what personality is to the individual (Sperry 2002). While an organization's culture is oftentimes difficult to describe, those in the organization can feel or sense it. Three aspects of a culture are notable. There is a cognitive aspect that reflects how members of the organization think and are expected to think about specific issues. There is an affective or emotional aspect that reflects how members of the organization feel and are expected to feel about matters. And there is a behavioral aspect that reflects how things are to be done in the organization.

Much has been written lately about the Church's culture and its far-reaching impact on individual members. At least three types of Church culture can be described: ecclesial, clerical, and episcopal. Ecclesial culture refers to the values, behaviors, and actions associated with the institutional Church, in terms of diocese, religious orders, and the Vatican. The dark side of ecclesial culture is characterized by denial, evasion, secrecy, and status (Cozzens 2002:88). Clerical culture refers to the values, behaviors, and actions associated not only with the ordained clergy but also in some nonordained individuals working at the parish or diocesan level who identify strongly with clergy. The clerical culture is characterized by privilege, separateness, status, and entitlement with its attendant upside and downside. The downside of such a culture is that it can foster a sense of narcissistic entitlement and self-absorption and "tended to keep priests emotionally immature and excessively dependent on the approval of their superiors and parishioners" (Cozzens 2002:115). Clericalism, which is a dysfunctional form of this culture, is notable for its "authoritarian style of ministerial leadership, a rigidly hierarchical world view and a virtual identification of the holiness and grace of the church with the clerical state and, thereby, with the cleric himself" (p. 118). Episcopal culture is a variant of clerical culture reflected in the values and behaviors associated with bishops and cardinals. The upside of this culture is wisdom and humility, while the downside is entitlement, arrogance, and a lack of respect and accountability.

To the extent to which ecclesial, clerical, and episcopal cultures reflect entitlement, denial, arrogance, a lack of respect and accountability, and self-absorption, these cultures foster abusiveness. Accordingly, the culture of some religious organizations can be characterized as entitlement and abuse-prone. Abuse-proneness refers to organizational dynamics that promote and condone abusiveness and its expression. The impact of such a culture can and does have differential effects on different individuals. For example, such an entitled and abuse-prone culture would more likely foster sexual acting-out in ministers with lower levels of psychosexual development than in those with higher levels. It may be that priests with low levels of psychosexual development and high levels of narcissistic entitlement or even narcissistic and/or antisocial personality disorders will act out sexually even when the diocese or religious order's ecclesial culture is not particularly abuse-prone. On the other hand, there are situations wherein the ecclesial culture tolerates and "encourages" entitlement and abusiveness. Such circumstances can "tip the balance" such that a vulnerable but otherwise reasonably sexually and emotionally mature priest may engage in sexual impropriety when he is under considerable stress and fails to maintain appropriate boundaries in interpersonal relationships.

It should not be too surprising then that dioceses and religious orders with such cultures have had a much higher incidence of reported sexual misconduct than other dioceses and orders. Some have pointed to the Archdiocese of Santa Fe in New Mexico and the Irish Christian Brothers in Ireland and Northern Ireland as examples of cultures that appeared to have fostered, presumably unwittingly, abusiveness, particularly sexual misconduct.

Figure 4-2 indicates the relationship among types of clergy culture and levels of psychosexual development of priests.

Figure 4-2: Influence of Clergy Culture and Psychosexual Development on Priest Functioning

		Psychosexual Development	
		Low	*High*
Entitled/ Abuse-Prone Culture	*Non- Supportive*	Marginal Priests	Sexually Integrated and Satisfied Priests
	Tacitly Supportive	Abuse-Prone Priests	Sexually Integrated but Dissatisfied Priests

It is noteworthy that Curt's religious order manifests a burnout-prone culture. And it is interesting to speculate that such a culture is actually a variant of the abuse-prone culture. It is abuse-prone in that such burnout-prone cultures actually, but unwittingly, allow their own members to be physically and emotionally abused by the demands of ministry. Accordingly, Curt could be considered a sexually abuse-prone priest, but because of his asexual orientation he committed no overt sexual misconduct.

Ministry Assignment

Specific demands and expectations related to a pastoral assignment can account for considerable stress, depending on a number of factors. Fortunately, these stresses can be neutralized by the support systems in a minister's job environment or living situation. Curt's central-city parish had once been one of the wealthiest in the diocese. Now the congregation's membership was less than one-half of what it had been during its heyday, and its collections and income were less than one-fourth. Typically, Curt's schedule included fifteen-hour days, seven days a week. Besides his sacramental responsibilities, Curt focused most of his energy and time on trying to help his elderly and otherwise disenfranchised parishioners obtain food and shelter and addressing other human-rights issues. He admitted that he assumed too much responsibility and had difficulty delegating tasks and saying no. This ministry assignment had been exhilarating to him for approximately two years but was now becoming a burden. The pastoral team consisted of seven full-time individuals, including two religious sisters, one layperson, and three other priests of Curt's order. All the priests had schedules about as hectic as Curt's. Although the four priests lived in the same house, they rarely saw each other, and usually only at dinner. Not surprisingly, Curt reported feeling isolated and lonely. He had no time for hobbies, and it had been two and a half years since he had taken a vacation. He had only one close friend and saw that person irregularly.

Relational Dynamics

The quality and type of the relationships in the minister's life can be predictive of the minister's overall health and well-being as well as his or her propensity to engage in sexual misconduct. Rossetti (1994) notes that priests who engage in sexual misconduct with minors tend to develop relationships and enjoy spending time with minors rather than with age-appropriate peers. He surmises that such priests favor relationships with minors because they are more comfortable with younger individuals than with their peers where such relationships are more likely to be less satisfying and more superficial. On the other hand, meaningful peer relationships require a more mature level of intimacy and of psychosexual maturity. Irons and Roberts (1995) suggest that relationships can also be problematic for highly committed, hard-working ministers in demanding ministries. When their theology of ministry and the culture of their diocese or religious order favor intense, active dedication, they become more vulnerable to imbalance in their lives. Such imbalance means they are likely to neglect self-care as well as to cultivate and maintain meaningful and satisfying friendships with peers. Such ministers who are married inevitably experience relationship issues with their partners. Not surprisingly, such relational neglect can increase their vulnerability to sexual impropriety.

Relational issues become more complicated when boundaries are unclear, power is uneven, and type and level of intimacy are inappropriate in given circumstances. In the remainder of this section boundaries, power differentials, intimacy, and transference and counter-transference are discussed.

Boundaries. A boundary is a point of separation. For individuals, the basic separation or boundary is between self and others. A characteristic of early infancy is the infant's perception of no separation between self and mother. In the course of normal growth and development, it is expected that the self becomes better delineated and that a clear boundary between self and others develops and is maintained. This interpersonal boundary specifies the degree of intrusiveness that will be accepted in the relationship. In close, intimate relationships, commitment to the relationship is a basic boundary issue, as is the friend's relative commitments to his ministry, family, social friends, and the private space to be alone with one's thoughts and dreams without intrusion. Thus, disclosing a close friend's deepest secrets would be a violation of this basic relational boundary. Boundaries can be rigid, clear, or diffuse. Clear boundaries are considered to be healthy and functional, while rigid and diffuse ones are considered pathological.

Conversely, individuals who have grown up in families with diffuse boundaries are very likely to exhibit a poorly delineated sense of self and are also very likely to experience problems establishing and maintaining healthy boundaries with other individuals and with institutions. Thus, individuals with personality structures that are characterized by self-deficits and identity problems, such as borderline personality disorder, are likely to be victims of various kinds of boundary violations.

Professional ethical codes require that clear boundaries be established and maintained in doctor-patient and counselor-client relationships. Boundary violations occur when the counselor fails to set or enforce limits on the appropriateness of his or her own behavior or on the client's behavior. For instance, a boundary violation would occur if a therapist asks a psychotherapy client, who is an investment broker, for advice on a particular stock, or accepts sexual advances from a client.

In a previous chapter it was noted that boundary issues for priests are considerably more complex than for other helping professionals such as therapists, physicians, and attorneys. Priests, particularly those in parish settings, are expected to play multiple roles and engage in complex relationships with parishioners in which interpersonal boundaries can be easily breached unless the priest is aware of that potential and takes appropriate steps to diminish boundary confusion and safeguard the integrity of these boundaries.

Power. Boundary issues can become intertwined with power issues. Power includes responsibility, control, discipline, decision-making, and role negotiation. Interpersonal relationships continually involve overt as well as covert attempts to influence decisions and the behavior of the other person. Control or power issues are usually tied to issues of money, reward, and privileges. They can manifest themselves in more subtle ways, such as escalation of conflict or one-upmanship in efforts to regulate another person's behavior. The basic dynamic in interpersonal conflict involves who tells whom what to do under what circumstances. Power in interpersonal relations can range from positive to negative emotionally, and from laissez faire, to democratic, to autocratic politically. Essentially, power becomes a meta-rule for all decisions about boundaries as well as intimacy. Power can be shared equally or unequally.

In a professional relationship, such as minister-parishioner, the minister is accorded a power differential. Even if a counselor or minister espouses mutual collaboration and decision-making, the power differential still exists. In other words, the client or parishioner still has less power than the counselor or minister by virtue of role and status. When this power over the parishioner is misused, it can also confound boundary issues. For example, when a minister makes sexual advances toward a parishioner, this behavior would be considered both a boundary and a power violation.

Intimacy. Intimacy involves self-disclosure, friendship, caring, and appreciation of individual uniqueness. It entails negotiating emotional as well as physical distance between significant others. In either instance, the goal is to balance a sense of autonomy with feelings of belonging. When issues of affection in a relationship become a source of difficulty, they can be manifest in various ways ranging from complaints, such as "You don't understand my feelings," to "I'm being taken for granted." True intimacy, as compared to pseudo-intimacy, requires that clear boundaries and equally shared power characterize the relationship. For this reason, true intimacy is seldom, if ever, possible in a professional relationship, given that a power differential usually exists. Thus, ministers or counselors who believe they truly love their client or parishioner are deluding themselves and others who become convinced of it.

Finally, relationships become problematic when transference and countertransference are unrecognized and ineffectively handled.

Transference. Transference refers to the psychological dynamic of transferring feelings, behaviors, and expectations from early life, parent-child relationships to current relationships. For example, it may be that the intensity of a woman's feelings of closeness to and affection for a priest who offers reassurance and comfort following a loss may be more rooted in her past than in the priest's actual words of comfort. Generally speaking, transference is more likely to be operative in relationships that are emotionally intense (Becker and Donovan 1995).

Countertransference. Countertransference refers to the ministers' transference of their own early-life feelings into a present relationship. As with transference, countertransference can intensify and confuse the real and actual circumstances of a current relationship. For example, a young priest's intense feelings of loneliness and sexual desire can easily lead him to misinterpret an attractive female parishioner's flattery as indications of her love and desire for him.

Because intense emotions can translate into sexual feelings, it is essential that ministry personnel have sufficient training, experience, and supervision in recognizing and handling transference and countertransference. They must also be aware that loneliness, tenderness, and vulnerability stir sexual longings and arousal. Furthermore, they "should expect to encounter sexual reactions (in themselves and in others) in the course of their work" (Becker and Donovan 1995:24). Finally, they must anticipate the potential for boundary confusion and power differentials in the various relationships they become involved in, both within their professional ministries and their personal lives.

Concluding Note

The manifestations of a minister's health or impairment, including sexual misconduct, may be more obvious than their causes. Four types of determinants of ministerial health and impairment, including sexual misconduct, were described. It was suggested that a minister's level of psychosexual development and theology of ministry as well as assignment, organizational factors—particularly culture—and relational factors are often ignored as contributing causes of sexual misconduct. Therefore, it is unwarranted to attribute a priest's sexual misconduct as simply a matter of personal moral failure or a deficit in psychosexual development. Such thinking is akin to pointing to a speck in the priest's eye while failure to see the log in the religious organization's eye. This is not to suggest that priests as individuals do not have shortcomings but rather to suggest that the causes of sexual misconduct are multiply determined. Finally, it was suggested that a religious organization's structure and culture does impact the level of psychosexual development of priests. Hopefully, this chapter has sufficiently made the case that a broad perspective is needed to understand the determinants of health and impairment if the institutional Church and individual priests are truly to become instruments of healing and wholeness.

References

Becker, J., and D. Donovan. (1995). "Sexual Dynamics in Ministry Relationships." *Human Development* 16 (3) 23–27.

Cozzens, D. (2002). *Sacred Silence: Denial and the Crisis in the Church.* Collegeville: Liturgical Press.

Irons, R., and K. Roberts. (1995). "The Unhealed Wound." In M. Lasser, and N. Hopkins, eds., *Restoring the Soul of the Church: Healing Congregations Wounded by Clergy Sexual Misconduct.* Collegeville: Liturgical Press. 33–51.

Karasek, R., and T. Theorell. (1990). *Healthy Work: Stress, Productivity and the Reconstruction of Working Life.* New York: Basic Books.

National Conference of Catholic Bishops. (1982). *The Priest and Stress*. Washington, D.C.: United States Catholic Conference.

Rosetti, S. (1994). "Red Flags for Child Sexual Abuse." *Human Development* 15 (4) 5–11.

Soroka, S. (1986). "Organizational Design of the Church As a Primary Source of Stress in Ministry." *Social Thought* (spring) 19–29.

Sperry, L. (1991). "Determinants of a Minister's Well Being." *Human Development* 12 (2) 21–26.

Sperry, L. (2000). *Ministry and Community: Recognizing, Healing and Preventing Ministry Impairment*. Collegeville: Liturgical Press.

Sperry, L. (2002). *Effective Leadership*. New York: Brunner/Routledge.

he founded, that he was being terminated as pastor. In a contrite manner Duvall admits to his wife, who is the church's music minister, that he is a womanizer and wanderlust and insists that she not leave him. He becomes increasingly disturbed by the thought of her and their two children taking up with the church's youth minister. He pleads that she give him another chance, but she will not. As the story proceeds we learn that Duvall's father was an alcoholic riverboat gambler who deserted the family, and we observe his ambivalent attachment to his mother. Throughout much of the story Duvall is portrayed as a fast and smooth-talking preacher who charms others while stretching the boundaries of his pastoral authority to get what he wants. When he cannot have his way, he becomes calculating, menacing, and violent. With premeditation he drinks and kills the youth minister with a baseball bat in front of his estranged wife and kids.

Rev. Richard Ellenberger had recently been assigned as pastor to a group of three rural parishes where a laywoman had been the administrator for nearly two years. She was competent and well regarded by both the pastoral staff and parishioners. The pastorate had been open for nearly three years, so there was considerable relief and hopefulness among parishioners when the announcement was made that the pastor would serve the sacramental needs while the administrator would continue to focus on daily operations and finances. The pastoral team had taken pride in the fact that they had worked collaboratively and effectively together for nearly two years in the face of serious financial constraints and sagging morale since the former pastor had been removed because of alcohol problems. Although the pastor seemed somewhat aloof and difficult to approach, the staff and most parishioners made nothing of it. But they did notice that he regularly parked in the handicapped space nearest the main pastoral office. They also noted that, at meetings where food was served, he left his dishes for others to clean up. He also didn't seem to be very good about returning phone calls or doing hospital visits. But no one complained. At least initially. During staff meetings and in personal conversations he seemed ill at ease and noncommunicative, which was in stark contrast to the confident and exuberant style of the administrator. He quickly got the reputation of being eccentric and "following his own drummer." The administrator, however, was concerned that pastoral needs were not getting met. When she saw him before or after meetings and wanted a word on a pressing concern, he would shrug her off with statements like: "Don't worry your pretty little head over that," or "You should be at home making babies." Two days later she demanded a sit-down meeting with him. At first, he made excuses why they couldn't meet. Later, he wrote her a brief note telling her she was "a demanding bitch and better back off." She asked for an apology and he termi-nated her without an explanation and without due process. Needless to say, she felt stunned, hurt, and devastated. The next day she con-sulted with her attorney about a sexual harassment claim against the pastor and the diocese.

Abusiveness in Ministry

What is the common theme in these three situations? All three of these ministers exhibit a pattern of abusive behavior. Dutton (1998) calls this pattern of abuse the "abusive personality." Since DSM-IV does not formally recognize the abusive personality as an Axis II per-sonality disorder, the designation "abusive pattern" will be used here instead.

This abusive pattern is characterized by a predictable constellation of abusive behaviors. It is important to note that the abusive pattern is not simply a single or even occasional instances of physical, sexual, or emotional abuse. Rather, it is an ongoing constellation of abusive behaviors that characterize an individual's functioning in given cir-cumstances. This does not mean that those with an abusive pattern are abusive at all times and in all situations; rather, they act abusively in given situations and circumstances. Many individuals with this pat-tern can appear to function relatively normally much of the time. However, specific circumstances can and do activate this constellation of abusiveness. Research indicates that the abusive pattern is the out-growth of a particular personality structure and differentiates three variants of this structure (Landolt and Dutton 1997; Dutton 1998).

A basic premise of this book is that abusiveness is a predisposing factor in priest sexual misconduct. While abusiveness is a key inter-nal factor in explaining priest sexual misconduct, it is but one factor. Other internal and external factors are involved. Thus, while abusive-ness is a necessary condition, it is not sufficient for explaining the full range of sexual misconduct perpetrated by priests. Chapter 7 details a vulnerability model of sexual misconduct involving abusiveness as well as other internal and external factors. This chapter provides im-portant background information for that theoretical model in addition to describing the types of abusive behaviors and the abusive pattern, including its development and its manifestations. Before turning to the abusive pattern, it may be helpful to describe abusive behaviors and the various types of abuse.

Abusive Behaviors

Several types of abuse can be described, i.e., physical, sexual, verbal, emotional, and spiritual. Table 5-1 specifies these types and provides examples of each.

Table 5-1: Types of Abusive Behavior

Type of Abuse	*Descriptive Examples*
Emotional abuse	shaming, withdrawing, withholding approval, brandishing a weapon, menacing gestures, "cold shoulder" treatment
Verbal abuse	threats, teasing, harassing, humiliating or derogatory comments
Physical abuse	destruction of property or pets, hitting, scratching, spitting
Spiritual abuse	parents and teachers using threats, i.e., "God will punish you" or using guilt
Sexual abuse	unwanted touching, fondling, or other sexual behaviors

There appears to be a single, unifying dynamic among these types of abusive behaviors. So, while there may be different manifestations of abuse, they all have one goal or purpose: to achieve control over the way others think and feel. In short, abusers are overly preoccupied with control. They exhibit an ongoing pattern of dominance or the power of subjugation. Not surprisingly, others views these individuals as "control freaks." Generally speaking, individuals with an abusive pattern, including those who engage in sexual misconduct, are individuals who have become extraordinarily proficient in controlling how others think, feel, and act (Sperry 2000).

Interestingly, recent research suggests that emotional abuse is common to all other forms of abuse and that emotional abuse can serve as a proxy for physical and sexual abuse (Dutton 1998). For instance, an emotionally abusive gesture or comment may remind a battered spouse or a sexually abused child that he or she can be beaten or molested at any time. Emotionally abusive behaviors can be destructive and intimidating in and of themselves, but they can be even more devastating when accompanied by physical intimidation and sexual intrusion. This chapter will focus primarily on the manifestations of emotional and physical abusiveness, and chapter 7 will emphasize sexual abusiveness or sexual misconduct.

Development of the Abusive Pattern

The abusive pattern has been the subject of considerable research over the past two decades. Among others, Dutton (1998) has conducted clinical research in search of the psychological profile of men who are emotionally and physically abusive in heterosexual and gay relationships (Landolt and Dutton 1997). It appears that these research findings are translatable to ministry personnel. Dutton (1998) describes three common developmental factors in abusive males. Table 5-2 lists these factors.

Table 5-2: Developmental Factors in the Abusive Pattern

Developmental Factor
• insecure attachment style with parent(s)
• being shamed by a parent
• witnessing abusive behavior

The first factor is the experience of insecure emotional attachment with their mother or early caretaker. Their attachment was typically one of unpredictable emotional availability leading to feelings of abandonment, and later a demanding and angry approach to adult relationships.

The second factor is the experience of being shamed by a parent, usually the father or a father figure. Being shamed by the father is associated with an abiding sense of worthlessness and identity diffusion. Shaming can take several forms, probably the most common of which is parental verbal ridicule and the expression of disappointment in the child's behavior or performance.

The third factor involves the experience of witnessing an adult engaging in abusive behaviors. Usually this adult is a parent, and typically what is witnessed are variants of the adult's abusive pattern with one or more victims. The child may or may not have been the victim of abuse, but abuse must have been witnessed.

Based on his research, Dutton insists that no single factor is sufficient to form the abusive pattern. All three factors must be present simultaneously. If they are present they create the potential for abusiveness that is shaped and refined by later experiences, and it is highly probable that the male will engage in abusive behavior. Furthermore, the way these three factors are shaped by early and later experiences influences the nature and severity of the abuse perpetrated. For example, adult males who were severely physically abused as children and develop abusive patterns are highly likely to physically abuse others as adults. Similarly, those who were severely sexually abused as children are more likely to sexually abuse others than those with abusive patterns who were not so abused. Nevertheless, emotional abusiveness is common to all who have developed abusive personalities.

Recognizing the Abusive Pattern

It was noted earlier that individuals with abusive patterns are preoccupied with controlling the way others think and feel. Control can be thought of as spanning a continuum from healthy to harmful control. On the healthy end, control takes the form of positively influencing and developing another's potential. Individuals exposed to this form of control typically feel encouraged, challenged, or excited. On the harmful end of the continuum, control takes the form of restraining or discouraging another's potential. Individuals exposed to this form of control will experience a range of negative feelings from annoyance to betrayal. The feeling of annoyance is a response to another's efforts to get and control your attention. On the other hand, feelings of anger, fearfulness, hurt, and betrayal are responses to another's efforts to abusively control the way you think and feel about yourself. Thus, a useful way of recognizing the abusive pattern is by monitoring how you feel when you are around them and when things are difficult. In such situations, experiencing feelings of anger, fearfulness, hurt, or betrayal probably indicates the presence of the abusive pattern. Three variants of the abusive pattern can be described.

The Cyclical Pattern

These individuals are easily recognized by their cycling between explosive abusiveness and contrite behaviors. Of the three types of abusive patterns these individuals are the most troubled and troubling to work with in ministry settings. They may be quite intelligent or otherwise gifted but are difficult to get along with interpersonally, and are problematic to work with or to work for because of their tendency to be easily threatened, irritable, jealous, and fearful and to mask these affects with anger and direct or indirect demands for control. They also tend to set very high expectations for others, inevitably ensuring that things will go wrong. In addition, they may experience high levels of chronic trauma symptoms including outbursts, restricted affect, depression, anxiety, dependency, and the inability to calm and center themselves when they are troubled. As a result, they have a tendency to ruminate and then blame and project their inner turmoil and shortcomings on others. Typically, this erupts into explosive verbal or physically abusive behavior. Alcohol or other drug involvement can fuel this eruption. Many of these individuals will meet criteria for the diagnosis of Borderline Personality Disorder. The case example of Rev. Jeff Nielon illustrates the cyclical pattern.

The Psychopathic Pattern

Characteristic of the psychopathic type is the tendency to use abusive control to achieve any and all ends. And although these individuals have the capacity to quickly size up individuals and situations, they have considerable difficulty empathizing with others. They can be cold and calculating and direct their abusive behavior with precision: with a slight smile on their face they will whisper a threat or make a derogatory comment and move on as if nothing had happened. They are masters of denial and deceit but will "confess" when they are cornered or it seems advantageous. Emotional abusiveness is easy and effortless for these ministers. Alcohol use is common in the psychopathic type. Of the three abusive pattern types, they are the most likely to utilize physically abusive behaviors and also the most likely to have been severely physically abused as a child. Often these individuals will meet criteria for the diagnosis of Antisocial Personality Disorder, also referred to as the psychopathic personality. The second case example of Robert Duvall's character in the movie *Apostle* is an accurate portrayal of this pattern.

The Overcontrolled Pattern

These individuals are overcontrolled in the sense that, while they harbor chronic resentment, they control its expression under the guise of either appearing stoic and serious or constantly and superficially cheerful. They wish to be unnoticed and unbothered by the needs and demands of others, but at the same time they want to be around others.

Thus, they will attempt to please others and to avoid conflict, but also avoid feelings and be emotionally distant from others. Sometimes they appear to be eccentric. Nevertheless, they are easily irritated and threatened by others. When they act out abusively, others who do not know them well may be quite surprised. Emotional abuse is their favored strategy: withholding approval, giving the "cold shoulder," missing important deadlines, acting totally unexpectedly, or giving false hope. Alcohol or other drug involvement exacerbates this abuse pattern. Often these individuals will meet criteria for the diagnosis of Avoidant, Dependent, or Passive-Aggressive Personality Disorder. The case example of Rev. Richard Ellenberger illustrates the overcontrolled pattern.

Dealing with the Abusive Pattern in Ministry Settings

Abusive ministers can be incredibly hurtful and demoralizing to those who work with them and ministries invariably suffer also. There is a tendency for religious leaders to assume that psychotherapy or a psychiatric referral is the answer to the problem of abusive behavior. Unfortunately, while such referral may sometimes help, it is only one of many strategies for managing and preventing abusiveness. Chapter 11 discusses other strategies for managing and preventing abusiveness and sexual misconduct.

Concluding Note

This chapter has defined abusiveness, catalogued the various types of abusive behaviors, and described its developmental factors. Three patterns of abusiveness were detailed. The challenge for religious leaders and formation personnel is to prevent and manage abusiveness. Chapter 11 describes several such strategies. Of note is that abusiveness is a key internal factor in explaining priest sexual misconduct. Chapter 7 details a theoretical model of sexual misconduct in which abusiveness is one factor.

References

Dutton, D. (1998). *The Abusive Personality*. New York: Guilford.

Landolt, M., and D. Dutton. (1997). "Power and Personality: An Analysis of Gay Intimate Male Abuse." *Sex Roles* 37 (5/6) 335–59.

Sperry, L. (2000). "The Abusive Personality in Ministry." *Human Development* 21 (3) 32–36.

Chapter 6

Narcissism, Sexuality, and Sexual Misconduct

Trouble had been brewing for some time at All Saints Church but had recently erupted in this otherwise large, quiet suburban parish. Composed of a majority of retirees and young professional families, as well as a sizeable group of undergraduate and graduate students from a nearby private university, the parish had been relatively trouble-free since it was established. A civil suit brought against the parish and the diocese by disgruntled parishioners had unleashed a torrent of sentiment within the parish to replace the liturgy director, the parish council, and the pastor. The suit alleged that the liturgy director had engaged in sexual misconduct with young women in the parish, and that while the pastor and parish council had been apprised of the matter, they had failed to respond appropriately and in a timely fashion. The liturgy director was married, childless, in his late forties, and had been employed by the parish for four years. He had been hired after an exhaustive search to find someone with his credentials: a graduate degree in liturgy and successful experience with a large diverse parish. During his first few months at All Saints, his charm and wit had won over many skeptics, particularly among the older parishioners, who were not eager to replace traditional liturgies and devotions with the new. In a short time, he succeeded in commanding a sizable, loyal following. Nevertheless, his flamboyant manner led some to complain to the diocese and others that he be reassigned to a more "compatible" parish community. A subsequent diocesan report concluded that, while the parish's liturgical and paraliturgical services were within liturgical guidelines, the services were more like performances than occasions of worship. The pastor had and continued to support the liturgy director through these times. And on the surface matters seemed to have settled down in the second and third years in the job. While he had always dressed impeccably, in his third year, he became noticeably preoccupied with his appearance and signs of aging. He returned from an extended vacation with a new look: a face-lift and hair transplant. Before he had arrived at All Saints, the liturgy committee had consisted of a number of mature men and women appointed by the previous pastor. Shortly thereafter, the committee composition changed dramatically to include young, attractive professional women who became extremely loyal to its new director. When rumors surfaced that the new pastor had placed some limitations on the director because of the complaints of sexual impropriety and scandal, the liturgy committee members defended the director and turned on the pastor and parish council.

In this chapter and book "narcissism" is understood as a specific *style of responding* to others that is self-focused but not necessarily pathological. Accordingly, our use of the terms narcissism, "narcissistic personality," and "narcissistic style" is not intended to imply or connote mental illness or psychiatric disorder. Rather, narcissism refers to a stable behavioral trait or a style of personality in which two or more narcissistic traits are present, i.e., the narcissistic personality. However, when the term "narcissistic personality disorder" is used in this chapter it does refer to a personality disorder, which is classified as a psychiatric disorder. Common to all personality disorders is an inflexible and maladaptive pattern of inner experience and behavior that causes significant impairment or distress. This pattern is characterized by an inability or unwillingness to take responsibility for one's life, to cooperate and collaborate with others, and to transcend one's own self-interest (Cloninger 1993). In short, such individuals can make life difficult and even treacherous for those around them.

The music minister not only exhibits narcissism but also appears to meet diagnostic criteria for the narcissistic personality disorder. The reality is that individuals with a narcissistic pattern are attracted to ministries, particularly high-visibility ministries and positions of leadership. Furthermore, narcissistic ministers are becoming increasingly common in religious organizations, including parishes, religious communities of men and women, and in diocesan and other ecclesial offices. Unfortunately, narcissistic ministers create an incredible amount of havoc in their ministry assignments. Narcissism and the narcissistic personality is one of six most common personalities in clinical and religious settings (Sperry 1991; 1999).

Not all narcissistic ministers are the same, just as not all narcissistic politicians or executives are the same. Although much has been published about narcissistic psychopathology, relatively little has differentiated its variants or types, and even less has described these types in religious settings. Accordingly, this chapter describes three variants, from clearly pathological to relatively healthy, of this personality among ministry personnel. It emphasizes the psychological, religious, and spiritual, as well as sexual dynamics associated with the narcissistic personality. Before describing these dynamics, the link between narcissism and sexual misconduct will be briefly noted.

Narcissism and Sexual Misconduct

In the Types of Priest Sexual Misconduct that are described in chapter 7, five of the six types are characterized by some degree of narcissistic entitlement. A number of researchers have also noted that narcissism is a factor in clergy sexual misconduct (Benson 1994; Friberg and Laaser 1998; Lothstein 1999; Dukro and Falkenhain 2000). For example, in their article entitled "Narcissism Sets Stage for Clergy Sexual Abuse," Dukro and Falkenhain (2000) report that, in their cluster analysis of priests and religious who were sexual abusers, they found four subgroups were identified. Two of the subgroups were characterized by narcissistic features, one with a classic narcissistic personality presentation, i.e., charming, socially facile, and successful in ministry, while the other subgroup was more conflicted, hostile, and resentful. The authors conclude that their study "highlights the importance of narcissism as a factor increasing the danger that a person will be a sexual abuser" (p. 25). These authors also quote Bishop John Kinney's address to the National Catholic Education Association in which he indicated that an "attitude of entitlement is prominent among those clergy and religious who sexually abuse" (p. 25).

Entitlement, i.e., a claim for special treatment, reward, or privilege, is a key feature of narcissism. It is important to note that these authors are indicating that narcissism and narcissistic traits such as entitlement—and not necessarily the narcissistic personality disorder—appear to be operative in sexual misconduct. While some sexually abusing priests and religious may and do meet criteria for the narcissistic personality disorder, other priests who sexually abuse children are likely to meet criteria for dependent and obsessive-compulsive personality disorders (Rossetti 1996). In addition to whatever personality disorder may be present, sexually abusing priests and religious characteristically exhibit the narcissistic trait of entitlement.

Psychological Dynamics

Narcissistic ministers are typically heralded as individuals possessing great potential. Consequently, great things are expected of them, yet seldom is their full potential realized. While some of these individuals can be extremely effective ministers, eventually, and inevitably, problems arise. For one, their unceasing need for admiration and the exploitative nature of their relationships becoming irritating. And, as time goes by, their ministerial presence seems less than genuine, having a gamey quality to it. In their striving for success, they easily and readily manipulate others. Typically, it is significant stressors such as the onset of physical aging, career setbacks, and the increasing experience of the emptiness in their relationships that precipitate crises in their lives and trouble in their ministries.

Narcissists believe they must rely on themselves rather than on others for the gratification of their needs. They live with the conviction that it is unsafe to depend on anyone's love or loyalty. Instead, they pretend to be self-sufficient. But in the depths of their being they experience a sense of deprivation and emptiness. To cope with these feelings and assuage their insecurity, narcissistic individuals become preoccupied with establishing their power, appearance, status, prestige, and superiority. At the same time, they expect others to recognize their entitlement and specialness and meet their needs. What is particularly striking is their interpersonal exploitativeness, i.e., manipulativeness, deceit, selfishness, and other control-oriented behaviors. Narcissistic individuals live under the illusion that they are entitled to be served, that their own desires take precedence over those of others, and that they deserve special consideration in life (Sperry 1995).

It must be emphasized, however, that these characteristics occur with different degrees of intensity. A certain dose of narcissism is necessary to function effectively. All individuals exhibit some narcissistic behavior. Among individuals who possess only modest narcissistic tendencies are those who are very talented and capable of making great contributions to society. However, those who gravitate toward the pathological extreme give narcissism its pejorative reputation.

Narcissistic ministers occupy different positions on a spectrum ranging from healthy narcissism to pathological narcissism. Three types of variants of narcissism in ministers will be described. These descriptions have been adapted from the types of narcissism among executives and leaders developed by Kets de Vries (1989). For him the factors that distinguish between health and dysfunction are intrapsychic and interpersonal dynamics. The DSM-IV-TR makes the distinction in behavioral terms, listing nine criteria: a grandiose sense of self-importance or uniqueness; a preoccupation with fantasies of unlimited success, power, brilliance, beauty, or ideal love; a sense of specialness; a need for excessive admiration from others; interpersonal exploitativeness; entitlement; arrogance and haughtiness; being envious of others; and a lack of empathy (American Psychiatric Association 2000). Meeting five or more of these criteria suggests the DSM-IV-TR diagnosis of narcissistic personality disorder, while fewer than five suggests narcissistic traits. These types are: reactive narcissism, self-deceptive narcissism, and constructive narcissism (Sperry 1991; 2000).

Reactive Narcissism: Ministers exhibiting reactive narcissism clearly meet diagnostic criteria for the narcissistic personality disorder but also exhibit features of other personality disorders such as the sadistic, paranoid, and antisocial or psychopathic personality. While they appear to be charming and engaging, they can just as easily be cold, calculating, and ruthless. According to Kets de Vries (1989), these individuals suffer from severe developmental deficits. Normal development involves two important spheres of the self. The first is the tendency to obtain reassurance through recognition, praise, and admiration, called "mirroring," referred to as the "grandiose self," while the second is the tendency to feel powerful through identification and idealization of another, referred to as the "idealized parental image." Both of these are poorly integrated in the reactive narcissist. Phase-appropriate development in the early years did not occur in reactive narcissists. Frustrating experiences were poorly handled. As children, they acquired instead a defective, poorly integrated sense of identity and subsequently were unable to maintain a stable sense of self-esteem and a cohesive sense of self. To cope with such feelings, these individuals created for themselves a self-view of specialness, which was a compensation against a constant feeling of never having been loved by their parents. The internal world of these narcissistic ministers was very likely populated by traumatic and malevolent images they cannot forget and continually fail to master but to which they continually react.

Creating the illusion of uniqueness is one method of coping or mastery but a brittle one. This inner fragility impacts their dealings with the external environment. Any discrepancies between capacities and wants are likely to accentuate anxiety and impair reality testing. As such, these individuals tend to distort outside events to manage anxiety and to prevent a sense of loss and disappointment. Examples of such individuals are Hitler, Saddam Hussein, and Osama Bin Laden, and others whom Scott Peck (1983) calls "people of the lie," i.e., individuals whose actions appear to reflect a sense of evilness, and whom others refer to as "malignant narcissists"(Kernberg 1984).

Reactive narcissists who are in major positions of religious leadership can cause considerable trouble. They tend to surround themselves with followers who are sycophants. They exhibit little or no concern about hurting others in pursuit of their own interests and readily devalue others to underscore their own superiority. Because of significant empathic deficit in their personality structure, they have little awareness of or appreciation for others' needs and feelings. Projects are undertaken on a grand scale but are often doomed to failure because of lack of judgment and an absence of reality testing. And predictably, when things go wrong, they blame others.

Self-Deceptive Narcissism: The second type of narcissistic minister also meets the criteria for the narcissistic personality disorder but does not exhibit the extremes of cruelty and paranoia as the reactive narcissist. The self-deceptive narcissist experiences a rather different pattern of early childhood development. During early development these ministers were probably overstimulated or overburdened. One or both parents led them to believe that they were completely lovable and perfect, regardless of their actions and in spite of reality. Such children become the proxies of their parents, entrusted with a mission to fulfill many unrealized parental hopes. Needless to say, they became profoundly anxious because of the ideals of perfection given them by their parents and uncertain if they achieved these ideals. What may have appeared as indulgence on the part of the parents was actually the exact opposite. Their parents used the child to meet their own needs. The imposition of these exaggerated parental expectations greatly confused the child about his or her actual abilities, which led to the creation of their delusory beliefs about self.

Such unrealistic beliefs may provide the original impetus that differentiates the self-deceptive narcissist from others. In some instances, the child is unusually talented and motivated and is able to achieve the level of success consistent with the parent's exaggerated expectations. In other instances, the child has less talent or fewer opportunities and utilizes the exaggerated parental expectations as the basis for excelling in some area of endeavor. In general, however, the self-delusory quality of the unrealistic beliefs created by parents leads to problems. An exalted self-image is usually difficult to sustain in the light of external circumstances such as disappointment and failure. The overvalued image of the self-internalized from an idealizing parent can become more realistic after interactions with more honest and critical peers, but the vestiges of the traumas of early disappointments tend to be indelibly etched on the fragile and distorted concept of self. Accordingly, self-deceiving narcissists are likely to suffer from interpersonal difficulties stemming from their desire to live up to the now-internalized parental illusions of self-worth. Thus, their emotions are superficial and their behavior has an ideal-hungry quality. In short, they find intimacy difficult and they look for others to provide structure to their lives.

To sum up this section, it is important to underscore that self-deceptive narcissistic ministers are much more approachable than their reactive counterparts. They are not nearly as exploitative and are more tolerant of dissenting opinions. They also appear more insecure. They are wary of threats in the environment and attempt to avoid making mistakes. They are not as quick to devalue others, are more eager to please, and are willing to engage in deals and exchanges with their followers. Their style of relating can have a more collegial quality as compared to reactive narcissists who are more concerned with how to transform those around them. The self-deceiving type stems from exaggerated parental expectations and demands, while the reactive type derives from harsh and brutal parenting. Although there are clear differences in the origins and relational behaviors of both types, both are preoccupied and dominated by their grandiosity.

In theory it is easy to distinguish between reactive and self-deceptive narcissism, while in practice the distinction is more difficult to make. This is mostly due to differences in parental response toward the developing child. One parent might have taken a cold, hostile, rejecting attitude, while the other might have been supportive, thus resulting in different gradations or mixtures of narcissistic styles. In addition, instead of being frustrated when ambitious parental expectations were incongruent with external reality, the child may have striven successfully to bring their abilities up to their perceived capacity. Furthermore, learning experiences later in life could have had buffering or mitigating effects.

Constructive Narcissism: Constructive narcissists or narcissistic personalities do not behave in a reactive or self-deceptive manner, and because they meet fewer than five of the nine DSM-IV-TR criteria, do not qualify for the diagnosis of narcissistic personality disorder. They seldom distort reality or use primitive defenses such as splitting, projection, or idealization, and are less anxious and estranged from thoughts and feelings. Instead, they are willing to express their needs and take responsibility for their actions. They tend to be confident and independent thinkers, largely because of parental encouragement. Furthermore, they were helped by their parents to see things in perspective and to avoid scapegoating and other destructive ploys. But most importantly, their parents' expectations of them were realistic and balanced, promoting accurate reality testing. When disappointed, these ministers seldom act spitefully and are capable of encouraging others and engaging in reparative action.

Nevertheless, these ministers have learned the art of manipulation and occasionally act opportunistically. Still, they have the capacity to relate collegially with peers and those to whom they minister. They possess a high degree of confidence in their abilities and are highly goal-oriented. They will take ultimate responsibility for their decisions without blaming others when things go wrong. Still, they sometimes come across as lacking in warmth and consideration. Their sense of inner direction, however, gives them the ability to inspire others and create a common cause, transcending petty self-interests.

In summary, reactive narcissistic ministers tend to be ruthless, grandiose, and exhibitionistic. They seek to dominate and control and are extremely exploitative. Self-deceptive narcissistic ministers are less grandiose and exhibitionistic. They want to be liked and are much less tyrannical. Still, they lack empathy, are obsessed mainly with their own needs, and are given to being discreetly Machiavellian, that is, cunning and duplicitous. Finally, constructive narcissistic ministers are also ambitious, manipulative, and hypersensitive to criticism. Yet, they possess sufficient self-confidence, adaptability, and humor to be effective in a variety of ministerial situations and interpersonal challenges. Finally, because constructive narcissists are not personality-disordered ministers, they seldom create the havoc in their ministries that is the hallmark of the reactive and self-deceiving narcissists.

Religious and Spiritual Dynamics

The religious and spiritual dynamics of narcissistic personalities are predictable and unique. These dynamics are reflected in their image of God, their prayer style, and other religious and spiritual patterns.

Image of God: Because of their self-absorption, self-deceiving narcissists must creatively distort the precept to love God and neighbor to fit their pathological perspective. For them, God—and everyone else—exists for one purpose: to love and take care of them. Their basic spiritual deficit is a lack of awareness of grace and an incapacity for gratitude. Accordingly, they imagine God as an all-giving father who recognizes their specialness and responds with great favor (Sperry 1991). Not surprisingly, they tend to understand faith as a magical entreaty.

Prayer Style: Consequently, they believe God will do exactly as they ask in their prayers, with no regard to the kind of claim God has on them. For them, there is only one kind of prayer: the prayer of petition or demand. Prayer as praise, self-examination, forgiveness, or thanksgiving has little meaning for them. Some narcissistic personalities may have intense mystical leanings that pull them in the direction of mystical experience, including the occult. This is understandable in light of their sense of specialness and grandiosity. However, they are more likely to experience a hypomanic state of self-exaltation than a true mystical state. When prayers are not answered as they expect, they become narcissistically wounded and feel deeply rejected. As a result, they may reject God, becoming an atheist for an instant or forever, because God has let them down (Sperry 2001).

Other Spiritual Beliefs, Behaviors, and Practices: Spirituality provides a ready-made forum to reinforce and reconfirm their grandiose self. For the narcissistic personality, the notion of vocation as a "call" from God or as a sign of "being set apart" serves as further reinforcement and confirmation of their belief in their inherent specialness and superiority over others. The roles of minister, spiritual guide, or teacher provide a forum to exhibit that special call. Thus, the spiritual forum is first and foremost a performance where the audience or spiritual directee "mirrors," i.e., admires and praises, this personality. Essentially, the narcissist believes that the actual purpose of spiritual activity is "worship" of themselves (Sperry 2001)!

Narcissistic individuals are also likely to be insensitive to the suffering and needs of others. While they may help others in need and engage in acts of charity, they will do it only if their charitable deeds are noticed by others. If their efforts do not bring attention to them they won't make a donation, extend a helping hand, lend a listening ear, or for that matter, continue it when the attention and praise of others stops.

Sexual Dynamics

Sexual Attitudes: Recently, narcissistic attitudes involving sexuality have been the focus of research on what is termed *sexual narcissism*. "An individual with sexual narcissism is incapable of giving and receiving emotional intimacy because of low self-esteem, insecurity, and dysfunctional beliefs about relationships" (Apt and Hurlbert 1995). Such individuals typically manifest long-term and are unable to integrate sex and intimacy. Typically, they are preoccupied with sex and sexual activity and view themselves as being accomplished lovers. Characteristically, they exhibit a casual attitude toward sex and possess an inflated sense of their sexual skills. Nevertheless, they are dependent on significant others, yet tend to blame them for the sexual dissatisfaction.

Sexual narcissism has been conceptualized as a clinical construct that includes features of the narcissistic personality disorder as well as sexual dissatisfaction and boredom and the inability to experience emotional intimacy. Like the personality disorder, sexual narcissism shares the following features: entitlement, interpersonal exploitativeness, sexual preoccupation, and compulsivity, promiscuity, empathic deficits, and an inflated sense of sexual skills (Hurlbert and Apt 1991). Sexual narcissism can be assessed with the Index of Sexual Narcissism (Hurlbert et al. 1991).

Sexual Activity: Narcissistic priests tend to be preoccupied with appearance, particularly their physical appearance, weight, and fitness, their clothing, and their sexual performance. Sexual activity for the male with a narcissistic style closely reflects his beliefs and attitudes. Avodat Offit, M.D., a psychiatrist and sex therapist, reports on her extensive experience treating such individuals. She notes that such narcissists prize their bodies. "They stroke their penises with absolute affection and pride . . . they extend their handsome appendage to be kissed and fondled as though doing their partner a great favor. If not erect, they may regard a partner with some disdain and contempt for her inability to raise the thing" (Offit 1977:68). She insists that engaging in sexual activity with a male narcissist "can be an experience in sexual and emotional masturbation. Men praise themselves monotonously for the size of their organs, proficiency, longevity, and special skills in eliciting orgasm. They do not even ask questions. It is not, 'look at me, am I not the most wondrous of men?' but rather 'Be privileged to behold me, I am the miracle'" (p. 69).

On the other hand, Meloy (1986) views sexuality for narcissistic ministers as basically autoerotic. In other words, only their arousal, pleasure, and satisfaction are important and worthy of consideration. This autoerotic attitude may be consciously denied but will be seen in a pattern of transient and multiple sex partners. Paradoxically, the narcissist's search for the perfect body to mirror his sexual desire, as well as the desire to be young and attractive forever, can be accompanied by impotence. Without a physiological cause, the inability to achieve an erection may result from the narcissist's fear of dependency. Meloy points out that celibacy may support their autoerotic attitude, because they are allowed the freedom of sexual fantasy that has no limits or the imperfections, awkwardness, messiness, or inconvenience of actual contact with another person. Sexual images can be perfectly gratifying. Furthermore, Meloy contends that by requiring celibacy, Church authorities may be unwittingly sanctioning the narcissistic minister's preference for fantasy and sexual demands.

On the other hand, Offit (1977) disagrees with the assumption that narcissists frequently engage in self-stimulation with a flair, such as in front of three-way or ceiling mirrors. Instead, she notes that many narcissists regard such masturbation as an embarrassment and social and sexual failure. They reason, "Why should I do it myself when I can get someone else to do it for me?" Accordingly, they seek out others using whatever charm, cunning, and exploitativeness is necessary to achieve both the satisfaction they demand and the control and admiration to which they are entitled.

Exploitativeness and Coercion: The question might be asked: Is there a connection between narcissism and abusiveness? Definitely. In the literature on narcissism, the terms exploitation and coercion are used to refer to abusiveness and abuse-proneness.

Exploitativeness and coercion are not uncommon in sexual misconduct involving priests with narcissistic personalities. Theories and research on sexual exploitativeness have focused more generally on rape and date rape rather than specifically on clergy sexual misconduct. Nevertheless, there may be some generalizability of these findings, particularly to sexual activity between priests and adult females and males, and possibly with prepubescent and postpubescent minors. Research indicates that the sexual exploiter uses a variety of exploitative tactics besides or in place of physical force. These include using false promises, teasing, verbal threats, professing their love for the other, giving alcohol or drugs to disinhibit the other, etc. Research also indicates that sexual exploitation often continues following the sexual coercion or misconduct. Typically, this involves influencing the other to desist from retaliatory actions. Finally, research suggests that those engaging in sexual exploitation tend to have a dismissive attachment style, the attachment style most associated with those narcissistic personality disorders. Essentially, this means that, while sexual exploiters maintain positive attitudes about themselves, they hold negative attitudes toward others (Baumeister, Catanese and Wallace 2002). In addition, exploiters are skeptical about close relationships, exhibit low levels of intimacy, and instead desire to remain independent. Not surprisingly, they crave sex but not emotional intimacy.

Table 6-1 summarizes these psychological, spiritual and sexual dynamics.

Table 6-1: Dynamics of Narcissism in the Narcissistic Personality

Dynamics	Description
Psychological	
Basic Features	*narcissism:* a style of responding that is self-focused; in contrast to an inherently, inflexible and maladaptive pattern, i.e., *narcissistic personality disorder* characterized by entitlement, grandiosity, admiration, envy, low empathy, and relational exploitativeness
View of Intimacy	intimacy for the narcissists means being admired or adored or basking in the glow of another
Types	*reactive narcissist:* charming and engaging, but can also easily be cold, calculating, and ruthless
	self-deceptive narcissist: more approachable, less exploitative, and more tolerant
	constructive narcissist: self-confident, adaptable, ambitious, and can be manipulative, but is effective in ministry and causes less havoc than the personality-disordered reactive and self-deceptive narcissist

Dynamics *(cont.)*	Description *(cont.)*
Spiritual	
Image of God	God is imaged as an all-giving father who recognizes their specialness; faith is viewed as a magical entreaty
Prayer Style	primarily petitionary prayer rather than of praise or thanksgiving; some may have mystical experience that reinforces their sense of specialness
Spiritual Beliefs	vocation is viewed as a "call" from God and a sign of "being set apart" that reinforces their belief in their inherent specialness and superiority
Spiritual Behavior and Practices	the purpose of spiritual activity is "self-worship"; attracted to preaching and presiding roles in which they focus attention on themselves and "work" the crowd
Sexual	
Sexual Attitudes and Beliefs	sexual narcissism is the incapacity for emotional intimacy because of low self-esteem, insecurity, and dysfunctional beliefs about relationships; nevertheless, narcissists are preoccupied with sex; have casual attitudes toward sex and possess an inflated sense of their sexual skills
Sexual Behavior	preoccupied with clothing, physical appearance, and sexual performance; they may or may not be autoerotically focused, but only their own sexual arousal, pleasure, and satisfaction is of concern
Sexual Misconduct	predisposing factors include self-justifying entitlement, coercion, cunning, and exploitative behavior

Concluding Note

Priests and religious who engage in sexual misconduct may or may not meet criteria for a psychiatric disorder, such as the narcissistic personality disorder. Nevertheless, it is quite likely they will exhibit one or more narcissistic traits, typically entitlement and possibly exploitativeness. When several narcissistic traits are present, a diagnosis of narcissistic personality disorder may be warranted. Even with this personality disorder, such priests can be extremely effective in their ministry, at least for a time. Eventually and inevitably, problems arise. For one, their unceasing need for admiration and the exploitative nature of their relationships become irritating to others. And as time goes by, their personal presence seems less than genuine, having a gamey quality to it. In their striving for success, they easily and readily manipulate others. Typically, it is significant stressors such as the onset of physical aging, career setbacks, and the increasing experience of the emptiness in their relationships that precipitate crises they may interpret in spiritual and religious terms. To cope with such stressors, such priests become preoccupied with establishing their power, appearance, status, prestige, privilege, and superiority. Their entitlement and interpersonal exploitativeness become painfully apparent to others. Narcissistic priests tend to live under the illusion that they are entitled to be served, that their own desires take precedence over those of others, and they use tactics such as cunning and exploitation to achieve the admiration, control, and sexual satisfaction, always at the expense of others.

References

American Psychiatric Association. (2000). *Diagnostic and Statistical Manual of Mental Disorders, Fourth Edition-Text Revision (DSM-IV-TR)*. Washington, D.C.: American Psychiatric Association.

Apt, C., and D. Hurlbert. (1995). "Sexual Narcissism: Addiction or Anachronism?" *Family Journal* 3 (2) 103–06.

Baumeister, R., K. Catanese, and H. Wallace. (2002). "Conquest by Force: A Narcissistic Reactance Theory of Rape and Sexual Coercion." *Review of General Psychology* 6 (1) 92–135.

Benson, G. (1994). "Sexual Behavior by Male Clergy with Adult Female Counselees: Systemic and Situational Themes." *Sexual Addiction and Compulsivity* 1 (2) 103–18.

Cloninger, R., D. Svrakic, and T. Prybeck. (1993). "A Psychobiological Model of Temperament and Character." *Archives of General Psychiatry* 44:573–88.

Dukro, P., and M. Falkenhain. (2000). "Narcissism Sets Stage for Clergy Sexual Abuse." *Human Development* 21 (3) 24–28.

Friberg, N., and M. Laaser. (1998). *Before the Fall: Preventing Pastoral Sexual Abuse*. Collegeville: Liturgical Press.

Hurlbert, D., and C. Apt. (1991). "Sexual Narcissism and the Abusive Male." *Journal of Sex and Marital Therapy* 17:279–92.

Hurlbert, D., and C. Apt, S. Gasar, N. Wilson, and Y. Murphy. (1991). "Sexual Narcissism: A Validation Study." *Journal of Sex and Marital Therapy* 20:24–34.

Kernberg, O. (1984). *Severe Personality Disorders: Psychotherapeutic Strategies.* New Haven, Conn.: Yale University Press.

Kets de Vries, M. (1989). *Prisoners of Leadership.* New York: Wiley.

Lothstein, L. (1999). "Neuropsychological Findings in Clergy Who Sexually Abuse." In T. Plante, ed., *Bless Me Father for I Have Sinned: Perspectives on Sexual Abuse Committed by Roman Catholic Priests.* Westport, Conn.: Praeger. 59–86.

Meloy, J. (1986). "Narcissistic Psychopathology and the Clergy." *Pastoral Psychology* 35 (1) 50–55.

Oates, W. (1987). *Behind the Masks: Personality Disorders in Religious Behavior.* Philadelphia: Westminster Press.

Offit, A. (1977). *The Sexual Self.* Philadelphia: Lippincott.

Peck, M. S. (1983). *People of the Lie.* New York: Simon & Schuster.

Rossetti, S. (1996). *A Tragic Grace: The Catholic Church and Child Sexual Abuse.* Collegeville: Liturgical Press.

Sperry, L. (1991). "Neurotic Personalities in Religious Settings." *Human Development* 12 (3) 11–17.

Sperry, L. (1995). *Handbook of Diagnosis and Treatment of DSM-IV Personality Disorders.* New York: Brunner/Mazel.

Sperry, L. (1999). *Cognitive Behavior Therapy of the DSM-IV Personality Disorders: Highly Effective Interventions for the Most Common Personality Disorders.* New York: Brunner/Mazel.

Sperry, L. (2000). *Ministry and Community: Recognizing, Healing and Preventing Ministry Impairment.* Collegeville: Liturgical Press.

Sperry, L. (2001). *Spirituality in Clinical Practice.* New York: Brunner-Routeledge.

Chapter 7

Priest Sexual Misconduct with Children, Adolescents, and Adults

Rev. William "Bill" Graven, ordained for some three years, became involved with a thirty-one-year-old separated female parishioner who came to him for spiritual guidance. Shortly afterward, one of the priest's closest relatives died and in his grieving he became increasingly sad and lonely. She offered to help him and soothe his loneliness, which soon led to holding and caressing him and then to intercourse. After a week, his mounting guilt over violating his promise of chastity led him to stop their sexual liaison and end their "counseling" relationship. She quickly left the parish and he heard nothing from her or about her for years until receiving a call from the chancellor saying that she had filed a complaint of sexual misconduct against him with the district attorney and the diocese. In the twenty-year interim, he had served his various ministry assignments faithfully and was respected by his superiors and had no issues with either celibacy or chastity.

Rev. Gerald Eamons had been pastor at Holy Redeemer parish for nearly twelve years when allegations of sexual impropriety surfaced. The pastor had the reputation of being a "servant leader" to his congregation who always seemed ready to go the extra mile for any parishioner in need. His dedication, generosity, and competence were well known in the community but were not, in his estimation, sufficiently appreciated. This lack of appreciation only fueled Eamons' resentment of his parishioners and their seemingly unending demands. In the past five years he had short sexual liaisons with four married women. His self-justifying entitlement began these relationships and raised his self-esteem, but only temporarily. Then his inner turmoil and anxiety mounted and was relieved by stopping the current relationship. However, in a matter of six or seven months his resentment would peak and he would seek out another sexual relationship.

Rev. Tomas Aguilara had been a shining light for his scholarly activity as a faculty member and chairperson in the history department at a small Catholic college. He worked tirelessly advising students, mentoring junior faculty, and administering his department. He had no time for hobbies, family, or for friends and fellow priests. Driven by shame and self-loathing, he pushed himself hard to compensate for the increasing sense of worthlessness he felt. Last year, this feeling lifted when he fell in love with an eighteen-year-old male student he was advising. Though he rationalized that this fondling, mutual masturbation, and oral sex were not illegal and did not violate his celibacy, he nevertheless experienced some guilt. In time, he became increasingly depressed and isolated and obsessed with the sinfulness of his secret life. A similar experience with another male student had occurred two years previously.

On his return from completion of a residential treatment for sexual-abusing clergy, Rev. Jeffrey Wisniewski stopped his car at an interstate rest stop for a cup of coffee. A trucker gave him the eye, and within minutes the two were engaged in consensual sex in the extended cab of the truck. While Rev. Wisniewski had ostensibly been sent by his bishop for treatment of his ephebophilia, the treatment team soon learned that Jeff impulsively engaged in sexual behavior with both males and females of all ages when he was frustrated and overstressed. However, only a small number were adolescent males. Wisniewski had the reputation of being an excellent preacher and a creative although somewhat unconventional pastor. He gambled, dressed stylishly, drove fast cars, and was rumored to have been arrested twice for driving under the influence. He had held five parish assignments in a twelve-year period. Two of these assignments had been for only a year, presumably related to concerns over misuse of parish funds in one parish, and sexual impropriety in the other that led his bishop to send him for residential treatment.

Rev. Andy Sharff was the charming and charismatic pastoral minister at a diocesan high school who was placed on leave after allegations of sexual impropriety involving three male adolescents over some ten years. His sexual misconduct began soon after his mother's death during which time he become increasingly preoccupied with sexual desire and arousal. This led to sexual encounters with several adolescents over a period of some six or more years. While one of these relationships lasted at least four years, there were other shorter-term relationships. Some of these occurred simultaneously, unbeknownst to the boys who believed they were involved in a special, exclusive relationship with the priest.

At age 66, Rev. John J. Goeghan was convicted of sexually abusing a 10-year-old boy. He is alleged to have abused at least 130 other victims over the period of about 15 years during his active priestly ministry. The media has noted that, despite the apparent awareness of his superiors, the priest was moved from assignment to assignment after parents of his alleged victims complained. Court documents indicate that Goeghan showed little concern for his victims and little, if any, remorse.

These cases exemplify various ways in which priests engage in sexual misconduct. Some of these ways seemed to garner more media attention than others. For example, both the number of children involved and the predatory quality of John Goeghan's sexual exploits generated infinitely more publicity than stories like that of Bill Graven or Tomas Aguilara, probably because of societal aversion to the sexual abuse of young children, particularly by those who hold positions of sacred trust. The abuse victims or alleged victims, as they are typically called, are children, adolescents as well as adults. Although the media focuses primarily on pedophilia, or the sexual exploitation of children, the incidence of priest pedophilia is quite small. On the other hand, the incidence of sexual relations between priests and adults—male or female—is considerably greater, while the incidence of ephebophilia is more than pedophilia but considerably less than priest sexual relations involving adults. Only recently have the media, religious leaders, and the general public begun to distinguish among these three forms of sexual activity.

Even though pedophilia has high visibility with significant psychological, legal, and financial consequences, religious leaders have a need to understand and comprehend the dynamics of sexual involvement priests have with adolescents and adults as well as with children. Accordingly, this chapter provides a brief sketch of each of these three types of sexual misconduct. It also proposes a vulnerability model for understanding the internal factors involved in triggering and fostering misconduct and a useful typology for recognizing different manifestations of misconduct.

Background Information and Considerations

As background for the discussion to follow, it might be useful to define key terms, some of which are used commonly as being synonymous, but which are not.

Definitions. Review and differentiation of the following terms will help clarify the discussion that follows. Their definitions can be found in chapter 1, page 11: *sexual abuse (exploitation); vulnerability; sexual misconduct;* and *sexual harassment.*

Psychosexual Disorders. Definitions for the relevant topics to be discussed here, *pedophilia, ephebophilia,* and the *paraphilias,* are found in chapter 1, pages 12–14.

Sexual Misconduct. See the general definition in chapter 1, page 11. Three forms of clergy sexual misconduct can be described (refer to chapter 1): *pedophilia* (pp. 12–13); *ephebophilia* (pp. 13–14); and *adult sexual misconduct* (Sexual Offender, pp. 10–11).

At this time, there is no reported research on the incidence of adult sexual misconduct involving Catholic priests. It is of interest to note that some data is available for other Christian ministers. One source that is widely quoted is a survey reported by *Leadership* magazine in 1988, a publication marketed to Protestant clergy. Of the 300 Protestant clergy responding to the survey, 77 percent indicated they had been sexually inappropriate with someone other than their spouse, while 12 percent indicated they had sexual intercourse with someone other than their spouse while engaged in ministry (cited in Friberg and Laaser 1998:vii).

Disorder, Immorality, or Crime?

The manner in which one conceptualizes sexual misconduct influences one's attitudes and response to it. There are three ways of conceptualizing sexual misconduct. Sexual misconduct, particularly pedophilia, can be considered as a psychiatric disorder, a crime, or an immoral act. The media seems to focus largely on sexual misconduct as a psychiatric disorder or a criminal offense and less as an immoral action. If sexual conduct is essentially a disorder, then the focus should be primarily on treating the offender and the victim—the so-called personal focus and impact, and secondarily on seeking redress for the criminal and immoral action—the communal focus and impact. The extent of the communal impact of one priest's misconduct can be significant. For example, the number of individuals impacted by John Goeghan's sexual misconduct over fifteen or more years may involve several thousand or more individuals, including victims, victims' families, parishioners in the parishes in which the misconduct occurred, not to mention others with secondhand knowledge, i.e., from newspaper and television, who were scandalized or repulsed.

Some psychiatrists like Thomas Szasz argue that pedophilia is a crime and immoral act rather than a psychiatric disorder or disease. Szasz (2002) insists that "Crimes are acts we commit. Diseases are biological processes that happen to our bodies. Mixing these two concepts by defining behaviors we disapprove of as diseases is a bottomless source of confusion and corruption" (p. 54). He insists that in viewing a priest who sexually abuses a child entrusted to his care as "suffering from pedophilia implies that there is something wrong with his sexual functioning, just as saying that he suffers from pernicious anemia implies that there is something wrong with the functioning of his hematopoietic system. If that were the issue, it would be his problem, not ours. Our problem is that there is something wrong with him as a moral agent. We ought to focus on his immorality, and forget about his sexuality" (p. 59).

In actuality, pedophilia is all three: a crime, an immoral act, and a psychiatric disorder. Since pedophilia has both personal and communal impact, religious leaders are challenged to recognize and address the legal and moral dimensions in addition to the psychiatric dimension.

Sexual Misconduct in Priests: A Vulnerability Model

Currently, there is no consensus among researchers on the causes of priest sexual misconduct. There is also very little research on clergy sexual misconduct, and what exists are small and limited descriptive studies of personality and neurological attributes of offenders. Nor are there theories or derivations of theories that adequately explain such misconduct. Having such an explanatory model could facilitate both the treatment and the prevention of it. Having no explanation of why certain priests seem more vulnerable or predisposed to sexual misconduct seriously limits the kind of research on the topic. On the other hand, having such a model fosters the development of typologies and the generation of research hypotheses that can be tested.

A Vulnerability Model: Abusiveness and Compulsivity

In chapter 4 we indicated that a comprehensive model of clergy sexual misconduct involved four factors: the priest, his religious organization or community, his ministry assignment, and the nature of his ministry relationships. This section describes a model for conceptualizing one of the dimensions of clergy sexual misconduct, the priest himself. Chapters 5 and 6 have pointed to two key factors that appear to predispose or increase the likelihood that a priest will engage in sexual misconduct. Those factors were abusiveness and narcissistic entitlement. It was noted that narcissistic entitlement sets the stage for abusiveness and exploitativeness. This chapter makes the case that adding the dimension of compulsivity, i.e., the inability to control urges or impulses, to abusiveness further increases the probability of acting-out. In short, it appears that *vulnerability* to engage in priest sexual misconduct is a function of both abusiveness and compulsivity. In this section, abusiveness and compulsivity are briefly discussed along with their theoretical and practical implications. A typology based on this model follows.

Abusiveness. Sexual misconduct is essentially an aggressive or abusive act. The establishment of an abusive relationship gives the offender power, control, and dominance over the victim and provides a connection—or "union"—with a real person that serves to reduce the offender's feelings of isolation and loneliness (Lothstein 1990). Blanchard (1991) reports that the nature of clergy sexual misconduct closely resembles incestuous relationships and that issues of power, control, anger, and hostility—manifestations of abusiveness—play a central role in clergy sexual misconduct.

Chapter 5 described abusiveness in some detail. Abusiveness was defined as a constellation of abusive behaviors—physical, verbal, emotional, spiritual and/or sexual abuse—that characterizes the "abusive pattern" (Sperry 2000). It was noted that offenders are not abusive at all times and in all situations but rather only in specific situations and circumstances that activate the pattern of abusiveness. Common to all forms of abuse is emotional abuse that can serve as a proxy for physical and sexual abuse. For instance, an emotionally abusive gesture or comment may remind a sexually abused individual that he or she can be sexually abused or beaten at any time.

Underlying the abusive pattern is the theme of dominance or power of subjugation. The abusive pattern reflects a preoccupation with control. Offenders typically become extraordinarily proficient in controlling how others think, feel, and act (Sperry 2000). While abusiveness is a key internal factor in explaining priest sexual misconduct, there are other internal and external factors. In short, abusiveness is a necessary but not sufficient condition in explaining the full range of sexual misconduct perpetrated by priests.

Compulsivity. Sexual compulsivity refers to the loss of the ability to choose freely whether to stop or continue a sexual behavior. It also refers to continuation of the sexual behavior despite adverse consequences and that the compulsive behavior continues despite efforts to cease or reduce the frequency of these behaviors. Compulsive behaviors can be further exacerbated and reinforced by accompanying obsessions, i.e., obsessive thoughts (Bryant 1999). Compulsivity involving sex is sometimes referred to as *sexual addiction*. As it has come to be defined, sexual addiction refers to a pathological relationship an individual develops to any form of sexual activity that has become unmanageable and that progressively worsens and usually results in negative consequences (Carnes 1989). Some researchers question the theoretical validity of this concept because it has yet to be documented by research as an actual clinical condition (Hurlbert and Apt 1991; Hoffman 1995). Nevertheless, the concept has continued to be used by clinicians and is widely accepted by the media and the general public.

Theoretical and Practical Implications: Assuming that sexual misconduct arises from both abusiveness and compulsivity allows us to speculate about the implications of this model. First, there are various combinations of abusiveness and compulsivity. For example, one priest may exhibit more abusiveness than compulsivity, while another could exhibit equal amounts of both. Second, the various combinations of abusiveness and compulsivity will impact victims differentially. For instance, a priest with high levels of abusiveness and high levels of compulsivity is more likely to engage in predatory forms of sexual misconduct than those with other combinations. Third, it should be possible to establish a taxonomy of sexual misconduct based on different combinations of abusiveness and compulsivity.

Typology of Priests Engaging in Sexual Misconduct

In the behavioral sciences, it is common to spell out or articulate a theoretical model in terms of a contingency table, i.e., a visual aid for specifying the relationship of variables or concepts. Figure 7-1 is such a contingency table that compares the dimensions of abusiveness and compulsivity in terms of varying levels: low, moderate, and high on the horizontal axis (abusiveness), and low and high on the vertical axis (compulsivity). The result is a typology of six types of priests engaging in sexual misconduct.

Figure 7-1: Types of Priests Involved in Sexual Misconduct

Abusiveness

		Low	Medium	High
	Low	Type I	Type III	Type V
Compulsivity	High	Type II	Type IV	Type VI

This section provides a detailed characterization of each of these six types, designated as Type I to VI. As noted earlier, this typology is derived from the *abusiveness–compulsivity model* of sexual misconduct and is based on my clinical experience with sexually abusive priests over the past thirty years. Somewhat similar models have been described by Gonsiorek (1987; 1999) and Irons and Roberts (1995).

The reader should note that each variant of sexual misconduct involving children (pedophilia), adolescents (ephebophilia), or adults is possible for each of the six types. Thus, while predatory pedophilia may seem to be more commonly associated with Type VI, other forms are possible. For instance, there could be multiple adolescent victims in predatory ephebophilia, or in adult sexual misconduct, such as in the form called Don Juanism, where a priest may serially seduce several women (or men).

There are at least five factors that characterize each type: (1) personality and level of psychosexual development; (2) number of victims; (3) degree of planning, cunning, and intimidation; (4) extent of concern for the victims and remorse; and (5) prognosis change or rehabilitation.

Type I: There are two variants of this type. In the first, the priest tends to be naive and relatively healthy psychologically. Despite their psychological health, priests who have little ministry experience or have limited pastoral training in sexual impropriety can have some difficulty recognizing appropriate boundaries and ethical standards involving power differentials with parishioners, particularly in responding to sexual involvement in somewhat ambiguous situations, such as, for example, when a teenager begins to relate in adult-adult interactions with a priest or when an adult female that a priest is counseling says she has dreams or fantasies about him. When under considerable stress and in the context of such situations, the priest may become sexually or romantically involved. This may occur even though the priest believes that sexual behavior involving parishioners is unacceptable. In this variant there is typically only a single victim and the prognosis is reasonably good for these priests, unless they are characterologically naive, which, according to Gonsiorek (1999), means that they may be too psychologically "dense" to effectively deal with the complex boundaries issue confronting them. This variant is one of the more common forms of sexual misconduct; there is little or no planning or intimidation and considerable guilt and remorse.

In the second variant, the priest is better trained but is somewhat neurotic. Such priests develop a sexual or romantic relationship with a vulnerable individual during a particularly stressful period in their lives. Following a recent loss, such as the death of a parent, such priests, who are likely to be depressed and lonely and have limited support networks, may find a needy parishioner who can fill the emotional void they are experiencing. A common sequence is for these priests to make inappropriate self-disclosures about their loss and loneliness, leading to social interactions with parishioners and then to sexual activity. Curiously, Gabbard (1995) describes such individuals as being "love sick." The prognosis for this variant of Type I tends to be mixed depending on the degree of neuroticism.

Type II: Such priests tend to be hardworking and devoted ministers who have sacrificed their wholes lives for the Church. These priests are often in the middle or later stages of their careers. Over time they have experienced mounting resentment and anger due to the insufficiency of appreciation shown by parishioners and/or the chancery or their provincial for all their efforts. They also feel unappreciated, abandoned, inadequate, and increasingly socially isolated. As a result, they rationalize that life owes them something in return for their great efforts and sacrifices. Their self-justifying entitlement and rationalization "allow" them to violate sexual boundaries and then engage in sexual misconduct. This impropriety is typically followed by intense feelings of guilt and shame quelled by stopping the relationship and resolving to work harder. But this strategy is short-lived as they become increasingly resentful, since their ministry situation remains unchanged. Subsequently, their entitlement and rationalizations lead them to violating sexual boundaries again. Because this pattern continues every few years, there may be a number of victims. A variety of addictions, particularly substance-related addictions, gambling, and workaholism may be noted in these individuals. Some planning and intimidation is usually noted and there is little or no remorse for their misconduct. Usually, there are a number of victims involved.

Treatment prognosis in these individuals tends to be guarded, meaning there is some possibility for major change but that such change is difficult to achieve since it requires considerable therapeutic effort to restructure their narcissistic and obsessive-compulsive style as well as their "doing" theology of ministry. Lasting change often requires a change in their ministry assignment away from settings in which boundaries are problematic for them.

Type III: Priests characterized by this type are somewhat like Type II priests in that they are somewhat narcissistic as well as deeply invested in ministries that are often quite demanding. But unlike Type IIs, these priests have come to believe that the measure of their self-worth is the degree to which they sacrifice themselves for others. Not only do they attempt to meet their personal needs for self-esteem in their work, but their self-definition becomes synonymous with the success or failure of their ministry. In addition, there is little or no balance in their lives, and little or no self-care, so they have not developed hobbies, learned to relax, and fostered friendships and celibate intimacy. Their obsessive-compulsivity, their burnout-prone theology of ministry, and their narcissistic entitlement become a recipe for disaster. This becomes particularly noticeable during those times when they receive little recognition and validation from parishioners, their peers and their bishop. This lack of validation results in marked feelings of worthlessness and shame that become unbearable. Their isolative style further compounds their loneliness and disconnection and reflexively they may turn to sexual relations as a validation as well as a remedy to assuage their shame. They tend to rationalize their actions, insisting that they truly love their parishioners and will engage in some sex acts but not others so as to remain "technical" celibates. Unfortunately, a sexual liaison is unlikely to provide the emotional supplies and feelings of control they expect and demand. Accordingly, their isolation, desperation, and depression only increase. Masturbation may become problematic for them and further increase their sense of guilt and shame. In addition to their work addiction they may abuse alcohol or other substances.

Like Type II, there is some planning and cunning involved but less intimidation of victims. While there is considerable guilt, there is also considerable rationalization of their actions. Nevertheless, in contrast to Type IIs, they tend to be remorseful after their misconduct has been disclosed. Typically, there are only one or two victims. Treatment response and prognosis tend to be guarded and depend on the success of therapeutic efforts to effect change in their compulsive need for achievement, pleasing others, and/or self-entitlement.

Type IV: Such priests tend to have ongoing problems with risk-taking and impulse control. In addition to having problems with interpersonal boundaries, these individuals may engage in other behaviors, such as criminal activities, most notably speeding and use of illicit drugs, but also embezzlement, sexual harassment, etc. They come across to others as energetic and engaging with a certain charm and creative touch. Like Type II priests, these individuals exhibit a narcissism marked by self-justifying entitlement. Their sexual conduct occurs both within the religious setting as well as in the larger community. Despite their energy and creative ideas they find it difficult to sustain and complete projects, leading to dismay and consternation among both parishioners and superiors.

Notable—and quite different from most of the other types—is the fact that these priests exhibit little, if any, planning or cunning in their exploits. Needless to say, they often engage in multiple sexual liaisons simultaneously. These priests will sometimes show remorse for their actions but not always. Unfortunately, their prognosis and response to treatment tends to be poor, particularly when issues of impulsivity and risk-taking have not been resolved.

Type V: Priests characterized by this type tend to be quite charming and even charismatic. They are also quite grandiose, often believing themselves to be better preachers, fundraisers, and administrators than their peers. They exhibit a high need for control and dominance and easily develop a following of loyal supporters who predictably will fiercely defend them when charges of sexual misconduct surface. Furthermore, these individuals have no qualms about bending rules and regulations to fit their needs and circumstances, particularly with regard to their sexual needs. Notable about these priests is their choice of a victim who is usually a vulnerable, dependent, and utterly loyal individual whom they choose to meet their sexual needs. Not surprisingly, relationships with these vulnerable victims are often long-term.

Owing to their narcissistic entitlement these priests tend to be clever, skillful, and manipulative individuals who utilize intimidation as a last resort to keep their victims from disclosing the nature of their relationship. Remorse for victims is unlikely. Fortunately, the number of their victims is small. Unfortunately, their response to treatment and their prognosis is usually poor to very poor.

Type VI: This type includes two variants: priests who fit the profile of the sexual predator and those with severe psychotic disorders. While the number of priests in both variants of this type is perhaps the smallest, Type VI priests seem to garner considerable media attention probably because of the sheer number of victims or the bizarreness of the misconduct.

Priests of the sexual predator type typically engage in repetitive sexual misconduct with minors, i.e., pedophilia and ephebophilia, or even with adult victims. These priests typically use manipulation, intimidation, and sometimes physical violence with their victims. Of the six types, they are the most intentional and cunning in their exploitation. They display absolutely no remorse for their actions and typically blame the victim for provoking their sexual behavior. Unfortunately, treatment response and prognosis for the classic sexual predator is hopelessly poor.

Those with severe psychotic disorders and who engage in sexual misconduct are particularly problematic in that, if their psychiatric condition remains untreated or they are noncompliant with that treatment, they tend to seek to "manage" their illness by acting out sexually. If they happen to be delusional, their sexual activity may border on the bizarre. If they have bipolar disorder, they may be hypersexual, i.e., overly preoccupied with indiscriminate or compulsive sexual activity. They are also likely to exhibit annoying, overbearing, demanding, and impulsive behavior marked by poor judgment. The prognosis for priests with these severe psychiatric disorders is often dependent on their compliance and responsiveness to treatment, particularly medications. When compliance is low, prognosis is very poor. Fortunately, treatment responsiveness and prognosis can be improved with ongoing monitoring of these priests.

Table 7-1 summarizes these six types.

An Analysis of the Cases of Sexual Misconduct

Let's now return to the cases that opened this chapter and review them in light of the theoretical model of the Types of Sexual Misconduct. The case of Rev. Graven rather clearly represents Type I, while the description of Rev. Eamons' circumstances is characteristic of Type II. The circumstances of the case of Rev. Tomas Aguilara illustrate Type III. Furthermore, Rev. Wisniewski illustrates one variant of Type IV, while the case of Rev. Sharff represents Type V reasonably well. Finally, John Goeghan illustrates the predatory abuser characteristic of Type VI. These cases serve to illustrate and underscore an important observation: there is no single pattern or characterization of priests who engage in sexual impropriety or misconduct with children, adolescents, or adults. More specifically, priests who engage in pedophilic or ephebophilic behavior or have sexual relations with adults can reflect any of the six types.

Table 7-1: Six Types of Priest Involved in Sexual Misconduct

Type	Description
Type I	two variants: *naive* involving a single victim; no cunning nor intimidation; usually remorseful; good prognosis; the *mildly neurotic* who is similar to the "naive" but has a mixed prognosis
Type II	moderately to severely neurotic and self-serving, martyr-like older priests who feel unappreciated; narcissistic entitlement with some intimidation; a number of victims; little or no remorse; guarded prognosis
Type III	hardworking, self-defined by their ministry; some narcissistic entitlement and planning; one or two victims; much guilt and rationalization; possible remorse; mixed to guarded prognosis
Type IV	impulsive, energetic, and immature; constant boundary problems and violations of rules beyond sexual impropriety; narcissistic entitlement; many victims; no planning or cunning; sometimes shows remorse; poor prognosis
Type V	charming, grandiose, dominating, and draw loyal supporters to them; usually long-term relationship with a vulnerable victim; narcissistic entitlement with cunning and intimidation; no remorse; poor prognosis
Type VI	two variants: the *classic sexual predator;* psychopathic with narcissistic entitlement; many victims; utilizes cunning and intimidation and may physically harm victims; no remorse; extremely poor prognosis; the second variant is *psychiatric disordered priests,* i.e., those with psychosis or bipolar disorder who, when untreated or noncompliant with treatment, act out sexual delusions or are hypersexual; in such instances, their prognosis is very poor

Concluding Note

This chapter began with six reasonably common presentations of sexual misconduct perpetrated by clergy. After reviewing some basic vocabulary and background information on sexual misconduct, we described a model of priestly sexual misconduct. Based on this *abusiveness–compulsivity model* six types of priestly sexual misconduct were articulated in terms of five factors: personality, number of victims, extent of cunning and intimidation, degree of concern and remorse, and prognosis. Finally, the six opening cases were analyzed in terms of this model. It is hoped that this model and typology will be useful to religious leaders and those involved in both formation and treatment. Presumably, it will prompt others to propose alternate explanations, models, and typologies that will promote both research and theoretical development. It will be because of such new models and the promptings of the Holy Spirit that religious leaders, formation personnel, ministers, and laity can sustain hope in facing the many challenges still ahead involving sexual misconduct of children, adolescents, and adults.

References

American Psychiatric Association. (2000). *Diagnostic and Statistical Manual of Mental Disorders, Fourth Edition-Text Revision (DSM-IV-TR)*. Washington, D.C.: American Psychiatric Association.

Blanchard, G. T. (1991). "Sexually Abusive Clergymen: A Conceptual Framework for Intervention and Recovery." *Pastoral Psychology* 39:237–45.

Bryant, C. (1999). "Psychological Treatment of Priest Sex Offenders." In T. Plante, ed., *Bless Me Father for I Have Sinned: Perspectives on Sexual Abuse Committed by Roman Catholic Priests*. Westport, Conn.: Praeger. 87–110.

Carnes, P. (1989). *Contrary to Love: Counseling the Sexual Addict*. Minneapolis: CompCare Publishers.

Friberg, N., and M. Laaser. (1998). *Before the Fall: Preventing Pastoral Sexual Abuse*. Collegeville: Liturgical Press.

Gabbard, G. (1995). "Psychotherapists Who Transgress Sexual Boundaries with Patients." In J. Gonsiorek, ed., *The Breach of Trust: Sexual Exploitation by Health Care Professionals and Clergy*. Newbury Park, Calif.: Sage Publications.

Gonsiorek, J. (1987). "Intervening with Psychotherapists Who Sexually Exploit Clients." In P. Keller and S. Heyman, eds., *Innovations in Clinical Practice: A Sourcebook* 6:417–27. Sarasota, Fla.: Professional Resources Exchange.

Gonsiorek, J. (1999). "Forensic Psychological Evaluation in Clergy Abuse." In T. Plante, ed., *Bless Me Father for I Have Sinned: Perspectives on Sexual Abuse Committed by Roman Catholic Priests*. Westport, Conn.: Praeger. 27–58.

Groth, N., W. Hobson, and T. Gary. (1982). "The Child Molester: Clinical Observations." In J. Conte and D. Shore, eds., *Social Work and Child Sexual Abuse*. New York: Haworth.

Hoffman, J. (1995). "Response to Sexual Narcissism: Addiction or Anachronism?" *Family Journal* 3 (2) 108–09.

Hurlbert, D., and C. Apt. (1991). "Sexual Narcissism and the Abusive Male." *Journal of Sex and Marital Therapy* 17:279–92.

Irons, R., and K. Roberts. (1995). "The Unhealed Wound." In M. Lasser, and N. Hopkins, eds., *Restoring the Soul of the Church: Healing Congregations Wounded by Clergy Sexual Misconduct*. Collegeville: Liturgical Press. 33–51.

Laaser, M. (1991). "Sexual Addiction and Clergy." *Pastoral Psychology* 39 (4) 213–35.

Lothstein, L. (1990). "Psychological Theories of Pedophilia and Ephebophilia." In S. Rosetti, ed., *Slayer of the Soul: Child Sexual Abuse and the Catholic Church*. Mystic, Conn.: Twenty-Third Publications. 19–44.

Plante, T., ed. (1999). *Bless Me Father for I Have Sinned: Perspectives on Sexual Abuse Committed by Roman Catholic Priests*. New York: Praeger.

Rossetti, S. (1994). "Some Red Flags for Child Sexual Abuse." *Human Development* 15 (4) 5–11.

Rossetti, S. (1996). *A Tragic Grace: The Catholic Church and Child Sexual Abuse*. Collegeville: Liturgical Press.

Shriver, S., C. Byer, L. Shainburg, and G. Falliano. (2002). *Dimensions of Human Sexuality*. Boston: McGraw Hill.

Sperry, L. (2000). "The Abusive Personality in Ministry." *Human Development* 21 (3) 32–36.

Szasz, T (2002). "Sins of the Fathers: Is Child Molestation a Sickness or a Crime?" *Reason* 34 (4) 54–59.

Chapter 8

Selecting Suitable Candidates
for the Priesthood

While neither eliciting the level of passion and ideology of the debate on homosexuality, nor having the media appeal of priests being removed from active ministry for sexual misconduct, the issue of candidate selection for the priesthood is, nevertheless, timely and important. It is timely in that some have charged that seminaries are disproportionately discouraging or rejecting certain seminary candidates, i.e., candidates with conservative and traditionalist viewpoints (Rose 2002). It is important for at least two reasons. First, at a time when the number of candidates is small, the temptation to lower standards arises. Second, when budgets are tight, admission personnel or administrators can easily rationalize that detailed psychological evaluations are a luxury, and, while useful, they are not essential. Using similar reasoning, they might argue that, by assessing candidates' sexual history and psychosexual development themselves, they could further reduce costs given the high fees charged by consulting psychologists and psychiatrists. Such reasoning, we would contend, is a recipe for disaster.

This chapter focuses on three specific considerations related to the screening of candidates for the priesthood. First, it is presumed that a comprehensive psychological assessment is essential in the overall screening protocol for seminary admission and that such an assessment will be provided by a specially trained clinician. Second, it will be argued that a candidate's sexual history and psychosexual development is best assessed by an experienced clinician such as a consulting psychologist or psychiatrist. Third, because they lack a comprehensive theoretical framework for guiding screening decisions, even some of the best assessment protocols will manifest shortcomings. In this regard, an assessment protocol derived from the Integrative Model of Psychosexual Development, described and illustrated in chapter 2, is offered as an example of a comprehensive theoretical framework for guiding assessment and screening decisions.

Psychological Assessment in the Screening Process

The starting point for making decisions about screening and selection is to specify the purpose of screening and then design the screening process accordingly. Some believe that the basic purpose of screening is to eliminate candidates with the type of psychopathology or problematic attitudes or attributes that are incompatible with ministry formation and/or ministry service. These individuals view screening as having a protective function, i.e., protecting the ministry from potentially dangerous ministers. Others view screening as more formative. In the formative view, the "ideal purpose of screening is not to exclude candidates from ministry but to identify areas that need healing before active ministry can proceed (Friberg and Laaser 1998:13). After determining the purpose of the screening, the next step is to develop the assessment protocol.

We would contend that a truly comprehensive psychological assessment protocol is essential in the overall screening process for seminary admissions. Even though seminary and formation budgets are tight these days, there is little justification and the potential is high for accepting seriously problematic candidates when psychological assessment is eliminated or minimal. Such a minimal psychological assessment protocol might include only a single, objective psychological test such as the MMPI-2 and a brief interview to screen for severe psychopathology. Since standardized testing has been shown to be insufficient in assessing the potential for sexual acting-out among clergy (Plante 1999; Gonsiorek 1999), such a limited screening protocol is fraught with considerable risk. Neither is such a protocol sufficient to rule out neurotic tendencies and qualities antithetical to healthy, normal personal relationships in ministry.

Accordingly, a more adequate assessment protocol would involve both objective and projective testing and a detailed psychiatric interview that would include a full assessment of the candidate's psychosexual development and fitness for ministry. Such an assessment protocol would not only rule out severe psychopathology and neurotic tendencies incompatible with the priesthood; it should include "the kind of psychological information that also focuses on the particular and uniquely defining characteristics and personality of an applicant. We therefore believe that the following dimensions should be addressed by the designated psychologist when evaluating a candidate's readiness and availability for priestly formation" (Coleman and Freed 2000:16). These authors propose several dimensions they believe should be formally assessed. Table 8-1 summarizes these dimensions. It should be noted that, in addition to these dimensions, Coleman and Freed advocate the use of a battery of formal objective and projective psychometric assessment.

Assessment of Sexual History and Psychosexual Development

Few would disagree that a close scrutiny of the sexual history of candidates is an essential part of the screening process *prior* to a decision about admission to priestly formation. However, there are some who believe that such a psychosexual history is better taken *after* the candidate has spent approximately two years in formation, or before the candidate begins his year of pastoral experience (Coleman 1996). There are a variety of sexual history outlines or protocols of suggested questions that different evaluators utilize.

Performed by Formation Personnel or Trained Clinician?

While the time at which the history is taken and the type of questions asked are important considerations, perhaps an even more important consideration is *who* should take the history. There are two differing perspectives on this. One perspective is that admissions or formation personnel with some experience should take the history or ask the candidate to write the answers to a series of questions similar to those used in an interview format. The candidate then discusses his answers with a member of the formation team. The other perspective is that a specially trained clinician is charged with the responsibility of conducting an intensive interview of the candidate's psychosexual development.

Table 8-1: Psychological Assessment Protocol

(adapted from Coleman & Freed 2000)

Basic Psychological Factors

Biological and Constitutional Factors: health history and status; ability to actualize; family history of substance or psychiatric disorders; drug or medication history

Social Determinants and Current Life Situation: family background; educational and work history; friends and social support systems

Identity and Self-Concept: self-view and how viewed by others; level of self-esteem, ego-strength; personal and career aspirations

Personality Factors: capacity to work under tension and deal with multiple stressors; energy level; time management abilities; adequacy of defenses; cognitive functioning; presence and degree of underlying narcissism; capacity to establish and maintain interpersonal relationships; comfort and effectiveness in group settings; capacity for receiving feedback from others; empathic ability; capacity to maintain appropriate boundaries; ability to relate comfortably with authority figures

Sexual Maturity: sexual orientation, identity, and behaviors consistent with vocation; attitudes toward celibacy re: formational growth; potential resistance to growth and maturation of sexual experience or expression

Requisite Ministry Skills, Capacities, and Experience

Personal Capacities: openness and flexibility; sense of humor; capacity for self-appraisal; adequate physical health; decision-making skills; money management skills; adequate etiquette skills; adequate English fluency in reading, speaking, and writing; and familiarity with and attraction to the Roman priesthood

Interpersonal Capacities: adequate psychosocial development and capacity to relate to all age groups; the capacity for celibacy; and the ability to cope with loneliness and establish healthy, long-term relationships

Basic Ministerial Skills: leadership potential as exhibited in personal initiatives and personal life decisions; capacity to cooperate with others; capacity for active listening; capacity for compassion and empathy; and capacity to communicate adequately in English in both writing and speaking

Ministerial Experience: a commitment to promote social justice; past experience of active involvement in a parish or other Catholic community; familiarity and experience with ministerial requirements of the sponsoring diocese or religious order

Negative Predictors of Vocational Success
Emotional: self-preoccupation; poor judgment; inability to empathize; overly dependent, or overly defensive
Historical: previous treatment for serious psychiatric disorders; repeated failures; impulsive decision-making; decision based on intense spiritual experiences
Motivational: any indication that the candidate desires to escape "self," family, or life situation; attraction based on insecurity and wanting to be cared for; or ambitions that overreach one's capabilities

Some religious communities may find it compatible with their screening process to have the sexual history taken by a member of the vocations team or the formation team or to have the candidate write answers to a series of sexual history questions. Critics of this approach point to its shortcomings, most notably its validity and utility. Some have charged that this method of assessment is not taken seriously or is essentially useless. They point to some religious communities that go so far as to "coach" candidates on what and what not to say in the sexual history interview or in the written form they complete in order to gain admission to the seminary or religious community.

On the other hand, there are a number of seminaries that use experienced, trained clinicians to perform a psychosexual history, usually in the context of a comprehensive psychological evaluation. It is my belief that an in-depth psychosexual history that spans all stages of development should be done by an experienced clinician specially trained in performing such interviews. This format is superior to an interview and history taken by a clinician without special training and experience in taking sexual histories or one taken by a nonclinician. Stephen J. Rossetti, PH.D., a priest-psychologist who is currently the president of St. Luke's Institute, concurs and insists that clinicians who "screen candidates for ministry need to be trained in giving psychosexual histories" (Rossetti 1996:78).

Such experienced clinicians bring to bear not only sophisticated interviewing skills that allow them to ask nuanced questions and follow up on the candidate's responses to gather valid information. Such clinicians are also are attuned to the various risk factors and developmental indicators of sexual difficulties and easily identify them in the course of the interview, whereas "clinicians without this background can listen to the same interview and miss its significance entirely" (Rossetti 1996:78).

Contents of the Psychosexual History

Coleman (1996) presents a detailed interview format for taking a sexual history that was primarily designed by Steven Rossetti and Carmen Meyer. It covers eight areas and is briefly described in Table 8-2. Interested readers are referred to Coleman for the complete set of questions—sixty-six—and related follow-up questions.

Table 8-2: A Psychosexual History Interview Format
(adapted from Coleman 1996)

Area	Goals and Sample Questions
Family of Origin	**Goals:** to understand family attitudes about sexuality **Question:** How comfortable were family members in discussing sex and sexuality?
Prepubescent Sexual Development	**Goals:** to understand the individual's earliest sexual feelings and experiences **Question:** At what age were you first aware of sexual feelings or your own sexuality?
Sexual Abuse History	**Goals:** to determine if any sexual abuse or exploitation was experienced **Question:** When you were growing up, did anyone older than you ever touch you or look at you in a way that was blatantly sexual? (follow up)
Puberty and Adolescence	**Goals:** to understand adolescent sexual development, particularly regarding puberty and masturbation **Question:** What were your fantasies when you first masturbated? (follow up)
Sexual Orientation	**Goals:** to understand the individual's awareness of his sexual orientation **Question:** Have you ever been curious about or aroused by members of your own sex? (follow up)
Dating and Adult Sexual Activity	**Goals:** to understand the individual's experience of dating and adult sexual activity **Question:** Have you ever had a sexual encounter with someone you did not know before that day? (follow up)
Paraphilias and Problematic Sexual Behavior	**Goals:** to determine if the individual has engaged in sexual deviancy or problematic behavior **Question:** Did you ever engage in any sexual behavior that others consider to be unusual? (follow up)

Area (cont.)	Goals and Sample Questions (cont.)
Current Management of Sexual Behavior and Feelings	**Goals:** to understand how the individual manages and integrates sexual feelings in light of the celibate lifestyle of a priest **Question:** How do you understand and respond to your sexual desires? (follow up)

An Integrative Approach to Assessment

In chapter 2 case histories of three priests were analyzed in terms of the *Integrative Model of Psychosexual Development*. That model specifies several factors that reflect an individual's level of psychosexual development. We suggested that the seven predisposing markers can significantly impact development even prior to birth or much of early childhood. The other eighteen factors are primarily developmental indicators described in the context of four separate but interdependent lines of human development: biological, psychological, social, and spiritual. In light of this model and its various factors, it is reasonable to consider that such markers could be used in screening candidates for ministry, particularly for the priesthood.

Assessment of Developmental Markers

This sections offers another protocol for screening candidates. The proposed protocol is based on the *Integrative Model of Psychosexual Development* described in chapter 2. Briefly, that model specified stage-specific development factors and tasks for each of six developmental stages. Table 8-3 summarizes these stages and developmental factors.

These factors lend themselves to assessment in the form of related development indicators or markers. Table 8-4 specifies these developmental markers that are suggestive of developmental difficulties.

Following is a narrative description of the each of these factors along with indicators or markers of associated developmental difficulties, delays, or fixations.

Pregnancy and Birth Experience

Wanted and unwanted pregnancy. Children whose parents did not want or were ambivalent about the pregnancy may have more difficulty

Table 8-3: Developmental Factors by Stage

Stage	Developmental Factors
Predisposing Stage (prenatal to postnatal)	• pregnancy and birth experience • temperament and mother-infant "fit" • hormone levels • attachment style • history of abuse or neglect • family functioning and style • family attitudes re: sex
Childhood Stage (0–7)	• sexual self-exploration • self-soothing capacity • practice of adult roles • gender identity and parental identification • God-image • best friend or confidant
Preadolescence Stage (8–12)	• same-sex sexual exploration • homosocial play • heterosexual relational experience • sexual attraction feelings and fantasies
Adolescence Stage (13–19)	• sexual exploration or expression • sexual orientation • capacity for self-mastery • capacity for responsibility, cooperation and self-transcendence • capacity to establish physical and emotional intimacy
Early Adulthood Stage (20–39)	• capacity for mature intimacy • communicating about intimacy issues • capacity for critical reflection and critical social consciousness
Mid-Adulthood Stage (40–55)	• balancing self-interest with self-surrender • level of generativity • reaction to andropause

with self-acceptance than those who felt wanted and cherished. *Uneventful and problematic pregnancy*. Typically, problematic pregnancies involve significant stressors ranging from maternal physical or emotional abuse, illness or infections, smoking, drug use, etc., all of which can significantly impact fetal growth and subsequent development. Uneventful pregnancies involve regular prenatal care and none of the above noted stressors. *Birth experiences and complications*. The birth process can be peaceful and uneventful or stressful, i.e., birth complications ranging from premature birth, cord compression, caesarean birth, etc. Even subtle neurological complications can significantly influence hormone levels like testosterone and other neurohormones resulting in increased vulnerability to medical and sexual disorders.

Temperament

Temperament is an individual's genetically based behavior pattern of tendencies to respond in predictable ways. For all practical purposes, temperament represents the building block of personality with regard to activity level, emotionality, and sociability. Three main temperament patterns or styles are "easy," "difficult," or "slow to warm up" (Thomas and Chess 1977). These patterns persist through adulthood. Not surprisingly, individuals with "easy" temperaments are less likely to respond in negativistic, suspicious, or overly passive and dependent manners.

Attachment Style

Attachment is an inborn system of the brain that influences and organizes motivational, emotional, and memory processes involving caregivers. The impact of the process of attachment on development cannot be underestimated since the "patterning and organization of attachment relationships during infancy is associated with characteristics processes of emotional regulation, social relatedness, access to autobiographical memory, and the development of self-reflection and narrative" (Siegel 1999:67).

Attachment style refers to the patterns of emotional bonding between infant and mother, or other caregivers, which significantly influences the individual's ability to form intimate relationships in adulthood (Karen 1994). Distinct styles of attachment can be described. As discussed in chapter 2, the secure style is indicative of warm, caring and trusting relationships as compared to the three insecure styles: avoidant, anxious/resistant, or disorganized. The insecure styles are associated with less healthy and stable relationships as well as the self-regulation of

**Table 8-4: Markers and Associated Difficulties
by Developmental Stage**

Stage	Markers and Associated Difficulties
Predisposing Stage (prenatal to postnatal)	• unwanted or problematic pregnancy or birth complications • difficult temperament and/or poor mother-infant "fit" • abnormal hormone levels, i.e., testosterone • insecure attachment style • early abuse or neglect history • low family functioning and/or overly enmeshed or disengaged family style • overly negative or permissive family attitudes re: sex
Childhood Stage (0–7)	• inappropriate sexual self-exploration • limited self-soothing capacity • limited practice of adult roles • delayed or confused gender identity or parental identification • harsh or distant God-image • no best friend or confidant
Preadolescence Stage (8–12)	• inappropriate same-sex sexual exploration or precocious sexual activity • limited or no homosocial play • little or no heterosexual relational experience • limited or inappropriate sexual attraction feelings and/or fantasies
Adolescence Stage (13–19)	• inappropriate sexual exploration or expression • asexual arousal pattern or uncertain sexual orientation • limited capacity for self-mastery • limited capacity for responsibility, cooperation, and self-transcendence • limited skills in physical and emotional intimacy
Early Adulthood Stage (20–39)	• limited capacity for mature intimacy • difficulty communicating about intimacy issues • limited capacity for critical reflection and critical social consciousness
Mid-Adulthood Stage (40–55)	• difficulty balancing self-interest with self-surrender • low level of generativity • negative reaction to andropause

thoughts, feelings, and actions. Not surprisingly, insecure attachment histories are often found in those who engage in sexual misconduct or who have difficulty in achieving sexual health.

Level of Family Functioning and Family Style

Family competence refers to the level of functioning of a given family. Highly competent, i.e., healthy and mature, families show warmth, respect, intimacy, and humor along with the capacity to negotiate difficulties and maintain appropriate boundaries and have clear boundaries. Families with low competence—less healthy and immature—have problematic boundaries, confused communication, and either over-control family members or provide no structure or consistency. Family style refers to manner in which families relate to one another. For example, in the enmeshed or overly engaged style, families emphasize extreme dependency as well as closeness, and sameness in how family members think, feel, and act. On the other hand, in the disengaged style, families emphasize extreme independence reflected in relatively little cohesion and consistency in how family members relate to each other. Healthier families tend to have a high level of competence and a style that is interdependent, i.e., blends both the engaged and disengaged styles (Beavers and Hampson 1990). Needless to say, sexually problematic ministers often come from problematic families with characteristically moderate to severe levels of dysfunction and with family styles that are overly enmeshed or disengaged.

Family Attitudes Toward Intimacy and Sexuality

Parental attitudes toward intimacy and sexuality tend to be assimilated by the child. Thus, children whose parents hold reasonably healthy attitudes are less likely to have negative or ambivalent attitudes toward marriage and intimacy. On the other hand, parents can transmit unhealthy attitudes in their children and engender shame and guilt about sex and sexuality, or negative or ambivalent attitudes about marriage and intimate relationships (DeLamater and Friedrich 2002).

History of Early Abuse or Neglect

A history of verbal, emotional, physical, and/or sexual abuse in childhood or adolescence can significantly impact the individual's overall development in all spheres: biologically, psychologically, socially, and spiritually. Research increasingly demonstrates that early abuse negatively impacts normal brain development. It also suggests that adults who were emotionally and sexually abused as minors have a higher probability of sexually abusing minors than those without such experience of early abuse (DeLamater and Friedrich 2002). If it is determined that an individual being evaluated has an abuse history, it is essential to elicit the factual history as well as its impact on the individual both emotionally and physically. In addition, the evaluator must determine how the individual dealt with the situation and what resources he or she was able to draw on in coping or attempting to cope. Having an abuse history does not necessarily indicate that the individual's later life will be dysfunctional or disordered since the capacity to cope and the availability of resources largely determine the impact of the abuse.

Capacity for Self-Soothing

Self-soothing is the individual's own capacity to limit, minimize, and soothe painful affects such as fear or loneliness without recourse to emotional numbing, depersonalization, or derealization (Masterson 2000). In children self-soothing typically involves sucking a pacifier, thumb sucking, hugging a stuffed animal, self-stimulation of genitals, etc.

Parental Identification and Practicing Adult Roles

Somewhere between the ages of three and seven children begin forming the concept of marriage and long-term relationships. In favorable circumstances, the child begins to learn adult roles and expected behaviors through imitation or modeling. Accordingly, they then practice these adult roles and behaviors by "playing house." The child also begins identifying more strongly with a parent, usually the girl with her mother and the boy with his father, and this is often reflected in play as the boy "plays" the father and husband role and the girl the mother and wife role (DeLamater and Friedrich 2002).

Sexual Self-Exploration

Research suggests that the capacity for sexual response appears to be present from birth (Masters, Johnson and Kolodny 1982). Infants and very young children activate this capacity by exploring their sexuality at first openly, i.e., fondling their genitals, and then more discreetly as the child becomes aware of family and societal norms governing sexual expression. Some children will be severely punished for engaging in such exploratory behavior. Others will be ignored by their parents or caregiver and thus not learn societal norms regarding appropriateness of sexual exploration that can have long-term consequences. Related sensual experiences of infants and young children include being rocked, tussled, and cuddled, as well as sucking their fingers and toes, etc. Around the ages three through seven children learn about genital differences between men and women and exhibit considerable interest and curiosity in the genitals of other children and adults. Accordingly, this curiosity may be noted in such heterosexual activities as "playing doctor"(DeLamater and Friedrich 2002). Some parents will prohibit their child from touching the bodies of other children and may even restrict questions and discussions about sexuality, resulting in the child seeking information about sex from peers.

Forge Gender Identity

During early childhood and usually by the age of three, a child begins forming a gender identity, i.e., a subjective sense of what it means to be a man (or boy) or a women (girl). Simultaneously, the child is also socialized in gender-role norms of society, i.e., what constitutes maleness and femaleness, and how males and females are expected to behave (DeLamater and Friedrich 2002). Confusion or a significant delay in forging a gender identity may complicate later developmental tasks.

Best Friend or Confidant

A best friend is defined as someone with whom the child can risk sharing secrets, personal concerns, and dreams without being criticized or having the secret "breached." Usually this is a child of similar age and of the same sex outside the family of origin. The experience of developing such a confidant relationship presumes that the child has previously formed trusting relationships with family members, i.e., a secure attachment style, and is permitted to relate to nonfamily members and share confidential material. Overly suspicious and enmeshed families may be threatened by such sharing and may not permit such sharing. Not having such confidant relationships can negatively impact the development of mature intimate relationships in adulthood (Masterson 2000).

Homosocial Play, Sexual Exploration, Stimulation, or Activity

During the early phase of the preadolescence stage, children tend to congregate and play in separate or homosocial groups, i.e., girls separated from the boys. Such a separation means that sexual exploration at this stage tends to involve individuals of the same sex (DeLamater and Friedrich 2002). Some boys may engage in group masturbatory activity, i.e., "circle jerks," and other sexual exploration that is typically short-lived. For others masturbation may become a daily solitary ritual. Excessive sexual stimulation at this stage can be a risk factor for sexual problems in adulthood. Precocious sexual activity is a potential indicator of sexual abuse. Psychologically, the children in this stage begin to deal with body-image changes. Not uncommon among boys, locker-room comparisons are made about a boy's size, body type, and body hair. Unfortunately, such comparison may serve to confirm a boy's negative body-image and attitudes toward bodiliness and sexuality.

Heterosexual Relational Experiences

Also during the late phase of the preadolescence stage, boys will have the opportunity to be involved in heterosexual parties and group dating. While initially awkward, the experience of relating to their female counterparts is exciting and satisfying for most. Those who have limited access to such activities or choose to avoid them out of fear or lack of interest are foregoing a developmental opportunity that can have far-reaching consequences. Such heterosexual relational experiences are essential in developing a capacity for sustained, long-term intimate relationships (DeLamater and Friedrich 2002).

Sexual Attraction Feelings and Sexual Fantasies

Also during the late phase of the preadolescence stage, boys begin experiencing the onset of hormonal changes, secondary sex characteristics, and feelings of sexual attraction. Typically around ages ten through twelve boys begin experiencing sexual attraction and arousal to others, while it may be several more months to a year before experiencing sexual fantasies of others (King 2002). For most boys, this arousal and these fantasies involve females, while for others they involve males or both sexes. Individuals who report experiencing little or no arousal or fantasies in late preadolescence and in adolescence tend to exhibit other indicators of asexuality as adults.

Adolescent Sexual Exploration and Expression

Puberty is the early part of adolescence during which the individual becomes functionally capable of reproduction. A hormonal surge during puberty leads to heightened sexual interest. For most individuals, sexual experiences begin during this stage. These include sexual fantasies and genital exploration, e.g., masturbation, petting, intercourse, etc. The majority of adolescents begin to masturbate at least occasionally, and approximately 50 percent experiment with heterosexual intercourse, while between 5–10 percent of males and 6 percent of females report having sexual experiences with a person of the same sex (DeLamater and Friedrich 2002).

Arousal Pattern and Sexual Orientation

Arousal refers to the stimulation of sex organs as a result of erotic thoughts, pictures, or situations. Arousal can be objectively assessed in men by penile plethysmography, an instrument that measures penile arousal. Arousal may serve as a more reliable indicator of sexual orientation than "attraction" which is a somewhat vague term assessed by self-report. Based on arousal patterns, sexual orientation is based on the type, extent, and frequency of sexual fantasies and arousal. Four types of arousal are noted that translate into four orientations. Accordingly, the heterosexual orientation refers to arousal involving persons of the opposite sex, the homosexual orientation involves arousal by the same sex, and bisexual involves arousal by either sex. The fourth orientation is designated as asexual, in which there is no arousal to either sex. Asexuality represents the extreme of the underdevelopment of sexuality (Storms 1981). Accordingly, this fourth orientation is a useful designation since asexuality is not uncommon in priestly ministry.

Capacity for Self-Mastery

Self-mastery is the capacity to achieve a balance of pleasure and self-control over one's needs, desires, wishes, and cravings. This capacity reflects not only one's internal needs, developing sense of self, and personal discipline, but also internalization of such external factors as rules, moral standards, policies, and social norms (Masterson 2000). While the development of this capacity begins in childhood and extends into adulthood, it is during adolescence that the individual is challenged to achieve a level of mastery and focus over hormonal surges, sexual energy, and youthful enthusiasm. A limited capacity for such mastery can be associated with compulsive masturbation.

Capacity for Responsibility, Cooperation, and Self-transcendence

Responsibility or self-directedness is the capacity to control, regulate, and adapt behavior in accord with one's chosen goals, values, and external obligations without blaming, excessive procrastination, or avoidance. Cooperation is the willingness to work together with others to achieve a common purpose without limited effort, refusal, excuses, or intolerance. Self-transcendence is the capacity to move beyond one's own reality, i.e., needs and views, to acknowledge other realities such as God and the goodness of creation. The absence of two or more of these capacities is indicative of a personality disorder (Cloninger et al. 1993).

Capacity for Mature Intimacy

This is the capacity for expressing the self fully in a close relationship with a minimum of anxiety or fear of rejection. It requires the temporary suspension of personal boundaries while risking the sharing of one's deepest sense of self with trustworthy individuals. On the other hand, individuals without a healthy sense of self, such as borderline personalities, may engage in intimate behaviors and indiscriminately permit their interpersonal boundaries to be violated by those who are not worthy of such freely shared trust (Masterson 2000).

Capacity to Communicate Effectively Regarding Intimacy

The capacity to communicate effectively about intimacy issues presumes that the individual has reasonably developed communication skills (active listening and responding), as well as a reasonable degree of role-taking (presume role-taking ability), putting oneself in another's place, and empathy (feeling what the other is feeling without identifying with or feeling sorry for the other that is merely sympathy) (Bagarozzi 2001). It also requires the desire and willingness to communicate, share, and disclose personal information and feelings about oneself with a significant other. This capacity is facilitated by a secure attachment style, having parents and other role models who were effective communicators, and a reasonably high degree of self-esteem. Needless to say, these various prerequisites suggest that this capacity is limited in many individuals.

Capacity to Balance Self-Interest with Self-Surrender

Self-surrender is the capacity to forego egocentric self-interests that can be obstacles to acting with caring and compassion. It requires subordinating one's needs and desires and putting others' needs first (Sperry 2001).

Capacity for Critical Reflection and Critical Social Consciousness

Critical reflection is the capacity to objectively and systematically analyze ideals, ideologies, and assumptions, and then compare, contrast, and develop alternative explanations. *Critical social consciousness* is the capacity to analyze social and organizational situations and dynamics in terms of ethical and moral assumptions and consequences (Sperry 2002).

Level of Generativity

Generativity is the capacity to show concern for and interest in others, particularly in guiding and encouraging those in younger generations. Individuals with high levels of generativity often serve as mentors or volunteer their time and expertise, while those with low levels tend to be self-absorbed and relatively uninterested in the plight of others (DeLamater and Friedrich 2002).

Reaction to Andropause

Andropause is the male equivalent of menopause. Unlike women, where there is a sudden loss of hormones, men experience a gradual decline in testosterone starting after age forty (DeLamater and Friedrich 2002). But psychosocial factors predominate in response to inability to achieve earlier career goals, concerns about aging and loss of youthful looks, energy, or loss or changes in intimate relationships.

Patterns Indicative of Sexual Misconduct of Minors

While markers are specific reflections of problems or difficulties at a given developmental stage, in and of themselves, they are not particularly useful in making evaluative decisions, i.e., such as whether a candidate should be admitted to priestly formation or ordination. On the other hand, there are patterns of behavior that can be quite useful in developing a profile or in decision-making. In this regard, patterns reflect clusters of developmental markers. For example, a candidate who has few, if any, peer (age-appropriate) relationships, may exhibit some or all of the following developmental markers: inappropriate same-sex sexual exploration; limited or inappropriate sexual attraction feelings and/or fantasies; limited capacity for mature intimacy; difficulty communicating about intimacy issues, etc.

The question then becomes: What are the defining patterns—or profile—of priests who engage in sexual misconduct with minors? Rossetti (1996) has provided such a pattern or profile. He describes what he calls six "red flags" of sexual misconduct. These include confused sexual orientation, childish interests, and a lack of peer relationships. Table 8-5 lists and briefly describes these patterns. Added to Rossetti's sixth red flag or pattern, personality, is narcissistic entitlement and the narcissistic personality.

Table 8-5: Patterns of Priest Sexual Misconduct of Children
(Adapted from Rossetti 1996)

Patterns	Description and Rationale
confusion about sexual orientation	awareness and acceptance of one's orientation is expected to be achieved by mid-twenties but may be a few years longer for gays; thus, extreme naiveté, long-standing psychiatric illness, or sexual attraction to minors and related guilt and shame may account for confusion re: orientation
childish interests and behaviors	adults who sexually abuse minors are typically psychologically immature and tend to think, feel, and share the interests and activities of minors; thus, spending excess time and taking vacations with minors should be a major cause of concern
lack of peer relationships	sexual abusers of minors enjoy spending time with minors rather than their peers since peer relationships tend to be less satisfying and are likely to be superficial or stereotypic; since intimate and such meaningful peer relations reflect psychological maturity, the lack of such relationships is strongly diagnostic
extremes of sexual expression	a history of hyposexuality or lack of interest regarding sexual explorations and behaviors is as problematic as a history of hypersexuality or compulsive acting-out
history of childhood sexual abuse or deviance	since up to two-thirds of priest sexual abusers have histories of being molested as minors, the presence of such history is important to note; in the absence of such an abuse history, look for other types of earlier deviant sexual experience: loose family sexual boundaries, pornography, engaging in sexual abuse involving children as a teenager, etc.
passive, dependent personality with narcissistic entitlement, OR narcissistic personality	priests with a dependent, passive, compulsive personality style or disorder with deference to authority and narcissistic entitlement, OR a narcissistic personality style or disorder, who are under considerable stress and have access to vulnerable minors, have an increased likelihood of acting-out sexually

Concluding Note

The issue of candidate selection for priestly formation and for ordination is a sensitive and complicated one irrespective of the perspectives from which it is viewed: pastorally, financially, or ideologically. This chapter has offered a comprehensive and systematic approach to candidate selection based on developmental considerations. While psychosexual maturity is not the only criterion for selection, it surely is one of the most important.

References

Bagarozzi, D. (2001). *Enhancing Intimacy in Marriage: A Clinician's Guide*. New York: Brunner/Routeledge.

Beavers, R., and R. Hampson. (1990). *Successful Families: Assessment and Intervention*. New York: Norton.

Bremner, J. (2002). *Does Stress Damage the Brain? Understanding Trauma-Related Disorders from a Mind-Body Perspective*. New York: Norton.

Cloninger, R., D. Svrakic, and T. Prybeck. (1993). "A Psychobiological Model of Temperament and Character." *Archives of General Psychiatry* 44:573–88.

Coleman, G. (1996). "Taking a Sexual History." *Human Development* 17 (1/2) 10–15.

Coleman, G., and R. Freed. (2000). "Assessing Seminary Candidates." *Human Development* 21 (2) 14–20.

DeLamater, J., and W. Friedrich. (2002). "Human Sexual Development." *Journal of Sex Research* 39 (1) 10–14.

Friberg, N., and M. Laaser. (1998). *Before the Fall: Preventing Pastoral Sexual Abuse*. Collegeville: Liturgical Press.

Gonsiorek, J. (1999). "Forensic Psychological Evaluations in Clergy Abuse." In T. Plante, ed., *Bless Me Father for I Have Sinned: Perspectives on Sexual Abuse Committed by Roman Catholic Priests*. Westport, Conn.: Praeger. 59–86.

Karen, R. (1994). *Becoming Attached*. New York: Warner Books.

King, B. (2002). *Human Sexuality Today*. Upper Saddle River, N. J.: Prentice-Hall.

Masters, W., V. Johnson, and R. Kolodny. (1982). *Human Sexuality*. Boston: Little, Brown.

Masterson, J. (2000). *The Personality Disorders: A New Look at the Developmental Self and Object Relations Approach*. Phoenix, Ariz.: Zeig, Tucker.

Plante, T. (1999). Introduction. "What Do We Know about Roman Catholic Priests Who Sexually Abuse Minors?" In T. Plante, ed., *Bless Me Father for I Have Sinned: Perspectives on Sexual Abuse Committed by Roman Catholic Priests*. Westport, Conn.: Praeger. 1–6.

Rose, M. (2002). *Goodbye, Good Men: How Liberals Brought Corruption into the Catholic Church*. New York: Regnery.

Rossetti, S. (1996). *A Tragic Grace: The Catholic Church and Sexual Abuse*. Collegeville: Liturgical Press.

Siegel, D. (1999). *The Developing Mind*. New York: Guilford.

Sperry, L. (2001). "An Integrative Model of Pastoral Counseling and Spiritual Direction." *Human Development* 22 (2) 37–42.

Sperry, L. (2002). *Transforming Self and Community: Revisioning Pastoral Counseling and Spiritual Direction*. Collegeville: Liturgical Press.

Storms, M. (1981). "A Theory of Erotic Orientation Development." *Psychological Review* 88:340–53.

Thomas, A., and S. Chess. (1977). *Temperament and Development*. New York: Brunner/Mazel.

Chapter 9

Homosexuality and the Priesthood

The past twenty years have been a time of unprecedented debate of the political, legislative, and theological issues involving sexual orientation, particularly about homosexuality. While this debate began taking place in professional forums, it quickly moved to theological forums. The recent publication of *Homosexuality: The Use of Scientific Research in the Church's Moral Debate* by Stanton Jones and Mark Yarhouse (Inter-Varsity Press, 2000) has opened this debate beyond moral theology and juridical circles to ministry personnel and inquiring churchgoers.

The context surrounding this debate is much larger than the issues themselves. An understanding of this context is useful in critically examining the debated issues. This chapter provides a brief sketch of this context and then summarizes the main points in the book by Jones and Yarhouse. The basic context for this debate involves ideology, science, and compassion. Each of these contextual factors is briefly described followed by a review and analysis of Jones and Yarhouse's position.

Ideology

Ideology is a systematic ordering of ideas, opinions, doctrines, and symbols that form a coherent philosophical outlook or perspective concerning how individuals, groups, and society should act. On the other hand, science is a systematic ordering of data and knowledge forming a coherent and reliable explanation of phenomena based on observation, experimentation, and rationality. At its best, science is the polar opposite of ideology. At its worst, science and ideology are hopelessly intertwined. The reality is that some overlap between science and ideology occurs, commonly with regard to considerations such as determinism (Sperry 1995).

Determinism. Determinism is the view that individuals have no free will because their choices and actions are caused by forces beyond their control. Needless to say, determinism is central in the ongoing debate about sexual orientation, primarily as an underlying assumption rather than a main topic of discussion.

There are three views of determinism: hard, soft, and indeterminate. Those who espouse "hard determinism" contend that responsibility for one's actions is an illusion, whereas those who espouse a "soft determinism" believe that causation is not compulsive and to act freely is not to act unpredictably. Those who espouse "indeterminism" believe that the self can influence causation (Sperry 1995). Today, the hard and soft determinists' view dominates debates involving sexual orientation.

For example, advocates of either the "nature" or "nurture" stance inevitably adopt a hard determinist position. They will claim that sexual orientation is entirely caused by biology or entirely by parenting and early life experiences. David McWhirter, M.D., a gay-rights advocate and highly respected psychiatrist-researcher, notes that there are relatively few hard determinists in the scientific community who believe that sexual orientation is totally biologically determined (McWhirter 1993). Among those hard determinists are Blanchard and Zucker (1994) who reanalyzed data from a 1981 study on sibling sex ratio and birth order and concluded birth order is the single most reliable demographic difference between homosexual and heterosexual males.

The soft determinist position, on the other hand, would hold that the origins of behavior, including sexual orientation, are multiply determined and involve some measure of "choice" or "decision." A basic premise of many contemporary approaches to psychotherapy and behavior is soft determinism. Accordingly, a soft deterministic view of sexual orientation is that it is a function of "nature" or heredity, "nurture" or environment, and "choice" or decision.

For many, the sexual orientation debate is basically a matter of genetics vs. "choice." This distinction is itself a manifestation of hard determinism. It is probably more correct to say that, while individuals have certain inclinations to homosexuality, bisexuality, or heterosexuality, the inclination is not a choice, but the individual has a choice to make about what to do with the inclination.

While from a scientific perspective, the origins of sexual orientation are still unclear; from an ideological perspective, there is little doubt. The psychotherapeutic and behavior change implications of ideology are clearly demonstrated. Gay affirmation therapy is espoused by gay-rights advocates. On the other hand, "reparative therapy" is advocated by the National Association for Research and Therapy of Homosexuality (NARTH). Advocates of this ideology contend individuals who have tried to accept a gay identity but were dissatisfied or distressed should be allowed the opportunity to receive psychotherapy to relieve their gender identity conflict. These two very distinctly different ideologies inform two very different psychotherapeutic treatment approaches.

Science

Underlying much of the debate on sexual orientation is the "nature-nurture" question: Are homosexuality and bisexuality the result of biology, i.e., hormones or genetics, or parenting? A common conclusion is: "Sexual orientation is not what one does but who one is." However, some advocates of gay rights who are well-respected scientists caution against reaching premature closure. McWhirter (1993) has reviewed the major hormone, genetic, and brain-tissue studies and concludes: "The most striking feature about these bits of evidence is that they seem to highlight the idea that the roots of sexual orientation, whether heterosexual, bisexual or homosexual, are multiple and variable. As long as there are questions being asked, some scientists will be proposing ways to find answers. There are certainly no clear-cut answers from biology yet, and there are few determinists who believe or even think all of the answers are to be found there." (McWhirter 1993:54). Today, nearly ten years later, current research continues to suggest that sexual orientation is not innate or biologically determined but rather multiply determined.

Constructionism. Besides determinism, the social construction of reality commonly complicates the enterprise of science. Social constructionism is a process in which an individual or group revises or "constructs" a new or different interpretation or meaning that provides a better or more acceptable explanation for a phenomenon (Guba and Lincoln 1994). Constructionism is often confused with scientific investigation. For example, in some published interviews and commentaries about pedophilia cases involving priests, pedophilia is described by some as a psychiatric disorder rather than as a criminal behavior, or as immoral behavior. Those who construct pedophilia as primarily or only a sinful or immoral behavior reportedly view confession as a reasonable corrective. The implication is that if it is a psychiatric disorder, the alleged perpetrator's actions are considered sick rather, or more so, than criminal. This presumably explains the common practice of making financial settlements to victims rather than pursuing criminal prosecution. Interestingly, society had only recently "constructed"—via the third edition of the *Diagnostic and Statistical Manual of Mental Disorders* (DSM-III)—pedophilia as a psychiatric diagnosis. Prior to that, pedophilia was considered to be a criminal or immoral behavior. Similarly, alcoholism, which had previously been viewed by many as a moral failing, also was constructed or ascribed to have a medical cause and thus could be diagnosed as a psychiatric disorder. With regard to constructionism and sexual orientation, it can be noted that the term "sexual preference" has been largely replaced with the more neutral designation sexual orientation because of the implication that preference meant personal choice.

Whether it is scientifically justified for pedophilia to be considered only, or primarily, a psychiatric disorder is a consideration that has raised little or no discussion in either the scientific or the religious community. Thus, it should not be too surprising that few understand or construct pedophilia as both criminal behavior and as a psychiatric diagnosis (Sperry 2002). Surprisingly, few seem to view it as all three: criminal, psychiatric, and immoral behavior. The following table illustrates the possible relationships between psychiatric diagnosis and criminal (or immoral) behavior. Since such constructions seem to reflect changing, subjective opinions more than established, objective, scientific findings, what validity, if any, do these constructions have in serious debates and discussions?

Table 9-1: Relation of Psychiatric Diagnosis and Criminal Behavior

		Psychiatric Diagnosis	
		Yes	*No*
Criminal (or Immoral) Behavior	*Yes*	I Both Psychiatric and Criminal	II Criminal (or immoral) Only
	No	III Psychiatric Only	IV Neither Psychiatric nor Criminal

Compassion

For me, compassion takes precedence over ideology in both debates regarding sexual orientation as well as in everyday dealings with individuals irrespective of their sexual orientation (Sperry 1995). That translates to mean that sexual orientation issues are best discussed in an atmosphere of respect, integrity, and fairness. This presumably would hold for those endeavoring to work therapeutically with individuals with sexual orientation issues. In other words, it seems that advocating a specific ideologically based treatment to all clients or patients is the antithesis of compassion and competence and may also reflect a hard determinist viewpoint about the etiology of sexual orientation.

Science and Ideology in the Homosexuality Debate

Some have advocated for the ordination of active homosexuals. Not surprisingly, scientific research studies are often cited in current debates about the morality of homosexual behavior. It is the improper use or misuse of science in these debates that has concerned Stanton Jones and Mark Yarhouse (2000) and prompted them to write *Homosexuality: The Use of Scientific Research in the Church's Moral Debate*. They intimate that both liberal and conservative Christians have a limited understanding of the scientific research on homosexuality and all too often make inaccurate assertions (e.g., "Science confirms that homosexuality is a genetic condition") or illogical conclusions (e.g., "Since it is impossible to reverse sexual orientation, being gay is a normal lifestyle variant") when drawing on the authority of science. Thus, they wrote this book to review the scientific literature critically and "explore the logic of how it might or might not be relevant to the ethical debate among Christians" (p. 28). A basic question that inevitably arises in such a discussion is: Who determines, and by what authority, what is and what is not a "misuse" of science and psychology?

These authors make no effort to conceal their assumptions and presuppositions in defending their biblically based, traditional Christian sexual ethic. "We will show persuasively, we hope, that while science provides us with many interesting and useful perspectives on sexual orientation and behavior, the best science of this day fails to persuade the thoughtful Christian to change his or her moral stance. Science has nothing to offer that would even remotely constitute persuasive evidence that would compel us to deviate from the historic Christian judgment that full homosexual intimacy, homosexual behavior, is immoral" (p. 12). As regards their scholarly stance, the authors consider their book to "be a case study in good scholarship conducted 'through the eyes of faith'" (p. 12).

They note that advocates have turned to "scientific" evidence in order to convince Church leaders that traditional Christian moral beliefs and judgments regarding homosexual practices must be wrong since these beliefs and judgments cannot be supported scientifically. The book is structured around the four topics that are at the center of the debate: prevalence, etiology, mental disorder, and changing orientation. Each of these topics is the focus of a core chapter in the book and each critically reviews the scientific literature as well as "explores the logic of how it might or might not be relevant to the ethical debate among Christians" (p. 29).

The Prevalence of Homosexuality. With regard to the claim that homosexuality is very common today, i.e., a prevalence rate of 10 percent or more of the general population, the authors cite studies suggesting the actual prevalence rate of 2–3 percent is more accurate. They discount arguments that the prevalence is really 10 percent when "exclusive" homosexual orientation, i.e., attraction only to same-sex individuals (2–3 percent) is combined with "predominant" homosexual orientation, i.e., attraction, for the most part, to same-sex individuals (presumably 7–8 percent). The authors present data from eleven national probability survey studies that do not appear to support this assertion, which, in the authors' opinion, is "based on a misinterpretation of deeply flawed research published by Kinsey" (p. 46).

They contend the arguments that homosexuality is common and therefore morally neutral or that homosexuality is immoral because it is rare are both specious since they frame the debate—based on scientific research findings—in such a way that makes the caricature of the traditional Christian moral position seem untenable. Whatever the prevalence rates, the authors insist that complicated moral questions can never be resolved with the citation of scientific data.

The Etiology of Homosexuality. Regarding the etiology of homosexuality, the authors review several psychological and environmental theories as well as biological theories, particularly the adult hormonal hypothesis, the prenatal hormonal hypothesis, and the genetic hypothesis. They chronicle various scientific efforts to estimate the genetic influence or heritability of homosexuality, the so-called "gay gene," and conclude that the best recent study of biologic etiology suggests that genetics may not be a significant causal factor (Bailey,

Dunne and Martin 2000). The authors conclude, after a critical analysis of the research on etiology, that the research is currently incomplete and thus inconclusive. Nevertheless, they concede that there is some evidence for psychological, environmental, family, and genetic influences and brain differences in the causation of homosexuality. Along with others in the scientific community, they support an interactionist hypothesis, i.e., some combination of nature and nurture appears to be operative in explaining sexual orientation. However, they contend that, while these factors may be *contributing* causes for a specific case of homosexuality, it cannot be concluded that one or more of these factors represent the etiology or cause of homosexuality.

The authors take particular exception to the claim that if research persuasively demonstrates that homosexuality is caused by factors beyond an individual's control—meaning that because of causative factors an individual is incapable of responsible choice—then it is wrong for the Church to condemn homosexual activity or the gay lifestyle. Even if, they assert, there is a predisposition for homosexual desires and actions that is outside the individual's control, "that does not constitute moral affirmation of acting on those desires. . . . At the broadest level all humans are heirs to a predisposition that we have not chosen and that propels us toward self-destruction and evil—our sinful nature. The plight of the homosexual who has desires and passions that he or she did not choose is in fact the common plight of humanity" (p. 181).

Homosexuality and the Question of Psychopathology. The authors next address the issue as to whether homosexuality is a mental disorder or whether it is a normal lifestyle variant. Acknowledging that professional mental health organizations, particularly the American Psychiatric Association, have declared homosexuality to be a normal lifestyle variant rather than a psychiatric disorder, the authors indicate that "the majority of psychiatrists in America . . . and around the world continue to see same-sex attraction as signaling a mental illness" (p. 115). They do conclude that, even if it is conceived as a normal lifestyle variant, it is a misrepresentation to suggest that homosexuals experience no more distress than heterosexuals. The authors cite research on the higher rates of depression, substance abuse, and suicide among some, but not all, homosexuals. Whether these increased levels of distress reflect maladjustment, social prejudice, or other factors has yet to be determined. Nevertheless, they suggest that there is clear evidence that "relational instability and promiscuity among male homosexuals must figure as problematic for Christians" (p. 181).

Furthermore, they suggest that this issue of pathology/normal life-style variant is irrelevant to the basic moral debate. The reason is that psychopathology and immorality are different realities, and although they can overlap at times, mental disorders such as PTSD and psychosis are not intrinsically sinful life patterns.

The Question of Changing Sexual Orientation. Finally, they address the matter of whether psychotherapy or other interventions can effectively change homosexual patterns. They summarily reject the so-called "scientific" conclusion offered by many that there are no effective therapeutic approaches to change gays into heterosexuals. Instead, they review research that demonstrates that focused therapy can effect a change "of modest size, approximating that for such vexing conditions as . . . pedophilia, alcoholism, and Antisocial Personality Disorder. Initial change may occur for only a minority, and relapses among those who change at all may be frequent, but that is not the same as saying that none can change" (p.182).

They concede that a profound change in sexual orientation occurs only infrequently. Nevertheless, a change in sexual orientation is irrelevant to being a Christian. The basic issue, the authors insist, is not conversion to heterosexuality but rather to chastity, i.e., not engaging in homosexual actions.

Compassion and the Debate

Even though it appears that the authors' reporting of the scientific literature is reasonably accurate and representative of published findings, the fact that religious and moral questions may be informed by scientific data but seldom settled by it renders scientific discourse on such matters uncertain and perhaps moot, to say the least. Earlier, a basic question was posed: Who determines, and by what authority, what is and what is not a "misuse" of science and psychology? This question has not been directly addressed by the authors. Not addressing the question is—in my opinion—unfortunate since there appears to be a circularity in the authors' use of data to disparage others' claims based on the same or similar data, a circularity that conceivably diminishes, rather than supports, credibility.

While Jones and Yarhouse contend that the current debate on homosexuality involves a "misuse" of science, it is probably more accurate to describe it as the worst of science, wherein science and ideology are hopelessly intertwined. At that point when there is some common ground reached on the issues of determinism and the social construction of sexual orientation, is it possible to untangle ideology from science? Only then is it legitimate and useful to consider how scientific findings can be brought to bear on the topic of homosexuality. It is unlikely that such a common ground can be reached outside an atmosphere of mutual respect and compassion. While these conditions may not be immediately forthcoming in the debate, it is imperative that they be held up as criteria in moving what is now a clearly ideological debate in the direction of a scientifically informed debate, and perhaps, even one day, in the direction of a true dialogue.

References

Bailey, J., M. Dunne, and N. Martin. (2000). "Genetic and Environmental Influences on Sexual Orientation and Its Correlates in an Australian Twin Sample." *Journal of Personality and Social Psychology* 78:524–36.

Blanchard R., and K. Zucker. (1994). "Re-analysis of Bell, Weinberg, and Hammerstein's Data on Birth Order, Sibling Sex Ratio, and Parental Age in Homosexual Men." *American Journal of Psychiatry* 151:1375–76.

Guba, E., and Y. Lincoln. (1994). "Competing Paradigms in Qualitative Research." In N. Denzin, and Y. Lincoln, eds., *Handbook of Qualitative Research*. Thousand Oaks, Calif.: Sage. 105–17.

Jones, S., and M. Yarhouse. (2000). *Homosexuality: The Use of Scientific Research in the Church's Moral Debate*. Downers Grove, Ill.: InterVarsity Press.

McWhirter, D. (1993). "Biological Theories of Sexual Orientation." In J. Oldham, M. Riba, and A. Tasman, eds., *American Psychiatric Press Review of Psychiatry*. Washington, D.C.: American Psychiatric Press. 12:42–57.

Sperry, L. (1995). "Sexual Orientation and Psychotherapy: Science, Ideology or Compassion?" *Journal of Individual Psychology* 51 (2) 160–65.

Sperry, L. (2002). "The Homosexuality Debate." *Human Development* 23 (2) 8–12.

Chapter 10

Decisions about Removing Priests from Active Ministry and Fitness for Ministry

In chapter 2, Rev. Andy Sharff was introduced as the popular pastoral minister at a diocesan high school who was placed on leave after allegations were reported that he had molested three male adolescents. Sharff had a reputation for being charming, gracious, and successful in his work. Because of his charismatic manner and wit, he was extraordinarily effective in raising funds for what he called "the best high school in the world." He was a high-visibility spokesman for the school and over the years developed quite a considerable following in the community. His sexual conduct began soon after his mother's death during which time he become increasingly preoccupied with sexual desire and arousal leading to sexual encounters with several adolescents over a period of several years. While one of these relationships lasted at least four years, there were other shorter-term relationships. Some of these occurred simultaneously unbeknownst to the boys who believed they were involved in a special, exclusive relationship with the priest. Despite such reports, most students, faculty, and parents were stunned by the allegations. Many immediately dismissed them and rallied to support the priest they had come to love and admire. Immediately, he was placed on administrative leave while the diocese investigated the allegations. During this time three other allegations surfaced.

It was in 1982, after Rev. William "Bill" Graven had been ordained for some three years, that he became involved with a thirty-one-year-old separated female. She had come to the priest for help with life, her marriage, and her future. At the prompting of his pastor, he referred the woman to a therapist. She began meeting the therapist but also asked to meet with Graven for "spiritual guidance." Although he lacked formal training in pastoral counseling and spiritual direction, he reluctantly agreed to see her. In time she started confiding her private feelings and fantasies to him. It was during this time that his grandfather died. His grandfather had been a surrogate father to him after his own father was killed in an industrial accident. After the grandfather's funeral, Graven's sadness and loneliness peaked. The woman offered to help him and soothe his loneliness, which quickly led to her holding and caressing him and then to intercourse. She told him that she had fallen in love with him and that he was God's answer to her prayers. After a week, his mounting guilt over violating his promise of celibacy led him to stop their sexual liaison and end their "counseling" relationship. She quickly left the parish and he heard nothing from her or about her until receiving a call from the chancellor saying that a charge of sexual misconduct had been lodged with the district attorney and the diocese. In the twenty-year interim, the priest faithfully served the parishioners at his various assignments. He was also respected by his superiors and had no issues with either celibacy or chastity. The news of the charge—even though it was soon dismissed by the district attorney—was unexpected and devastating. He couldn't comprehend either the charge or the bishop's decision to place him on administrative leave.

Reports of these and similar cases are not uncommon in the media today. In both cases diocesan officials placed the priests on administrative leave. In time they would make a determination regarding removal from active ministry or even laicization, i.e., removal from the priesthood. Even with the National Catholic Conference of Bishop's (NCCB) Charter, diocesan and religious order leadership are challenged to evaluate cases with divergently different circumstances as these two cases illustrate. The question is: How do these decisions get made, and what criteria are utilized in making them? This chapter addresses this question and proposes a set of decisional criteria, as well as some guidelines for making such decisions. It recognizes that the matter of determining whether to formally remove a priest from active duty is similar but somewhat different from the matter of determining if a priest is "fit" for ministry. In other words, there are a number of non-sexual behaviors, e.g., embezzlement, as well as less serious forms of sexual impropriety, e.g., voyeurism, that suggest unfitness for ministry but presently are not addressed in the charter and are not viewed as requiring formal removal from active ministry. The fact is that diocesan and religious leaders, as well as independent lay review committees, are charged with evaluating complex allegations involving issues dealing with both removal *and* fitness for ministry. Accordingly, this chapter addresses both matters: the first section focuses on removal from ministry, while the second section focuses on fitness for ministry.

Decisions Regarding Removal from Ministry

The formal decision to remove a priest from active ministry is a decision with far-reaching consequences for the priest, for those to whom he ministers, and for the diocese or the religious order. For the priest, the decision may mean the end of a satisfying career and perhaps the only career the individual has or will have. Since many accused priests are in midlife or close to retirement, the prospect of nonministry-related jobs may be limited. The increasing number of priests who have or will be removed from active ministry only worsens the current priest shortage, a source of increasing concern for parishioners and laity. Finally, the implications of removing priests from ministry are many for dioceses and religious orders. Just considering the costs in terms of finances and personnel is staggering to the imagination. In short, since the stakes are so great, it is imperative that religious leaders and formation personnel are sufficiently enabled in making decisions with such wide-ranging consequences.

A Typology of Clergy Sexual Misconduct

Chapter 6 included a description of various presentations of sexual misconduct in priests. A theory of sexual misconduct was proposed in which sexual misconduct was described as a function of the degree of abusiveness and the degree of compulsivity exhibited by a priest. Accordingly, six types of misconduct were derived and described. Table 10-1 provides a capsule summary of these six types. The discussion of the decision-making will be based on this typology as well as on decisional criteria described in the subsequent section.

Table 10-1: Six Types of Clergy Sexual Misconduct

Type	Description
Type I	naive or mildly neurotic; usually single victim; no cunning or intimidation; usually remorseful; good to mixed prognosis
Type II	neurotic and self-serving, martyr-like older priests who feel unappreciated; much narcissistic entitlement with some intimidation; a number of victims; little or no remorse; guarded prognosis
Type III	hardworking, self-defined by their ministry; some narcissistic entitlement and planning, one or two victims, much guilt and rationalizations; possible remorse; mixed to guarded prognosis
Type IV	impulsive, energetic, and immature; constant boundary problems and violations of rules beyond sexual impropriety; some narcissistic entitlement; many victims; no planning or cunning; sometimes shows remorse; poor prognosis
Type V	charming, grandiose, dominating, and draw loyal supporters to them; usually long-term relationship with a vulnerable victim but may involve others; much narcissistic entitlement with cunning and intimidation; no remorse; poor prognosis
Type VI	the classic sexual predator; psychopathic with narcissistic entitlement; many victims; utilizes cunning and intimidation and may physically harm victims; no remorse; extremely poor prognosis; this type also includes psychotic priests who, when untreated, act out sexual delusions and without treatment response have a very poor prognosis

Criteria for Removing Priests from Active Ministry

The following criteria can be used to guide decisions about removal or return to active ministry. These six criteria include behavioral, biological, moral, and spiritual indicators. Of course, the applicability of these criteria presume that allegations, charges, a conviction have triggered a review process regarding the question of removal or return to active ministry.

The six criteria are severity, treatment prognosis and response, addictions, opaque character, response to change directives, and ministry performance. They are briefly described here.

1. **Severity:** Severity of the misconduct is probably the most important decisional factor. Severity refers to the grievousness of the sexual

misconduct. It is a function of the extent of abusiveness *and* compulsivity of the sexual misconduct and is reflected in the number of victims; the extent of planning, cunning, and intimidation; the presence or absence of remorse or contriteness; and prognosis or rehabilitation potential. One gauge of severity is found in the ordering of the six Types of Sexual Clergy Misconduct ranked from least severe (Type I) to most severe (Type VI). The more severe Types, i.e., V and VI (Types of Clergy Sexual Misconduct), typically have poor to very poor rehabilitation potential and outcomes, while Type I tends to have much better outcomes.

2. **Treatment Response:** Treatment response refers to the outcomes of formal treatment. Even though prognosis is specified in the six Types of Clergy Misconduct, the actual treatment response is a function of the priest's motivation and efforts, as well as the superior's expectations and involvement. It is also a function of the diocese or religious congregation's capacity to monitor high-risk priests after completion of treatment. The priest's initial response to allegations or charges as well as his willingness toward and responsiveness to a superior's directives are important indicators. For example, defensiveness and defiance or unwillingness to comply with a superior's referral for psychiatric evaluation or for treatment of whatever type—inpatient, residential, medication, or individual or group therapy—often correlate with relapse and recidivism, or with failure to meet treatment goals if the priest eventually agrees to undergo treatment. While response to treatment is largely the a function of the priest's motivation and efforts as well as the adequacy of the treatment program, it is also a function of the diocesan or religious order's expectations, structure, culture, and resources to operationalize a follow-up treatment plan after discharge from a treatment center. Presumably, it has the commitment of major and local superiors and includes a relapse-prevention plan. Furthermore, it may require the capacity and resources to formally and regularly monitor a priest if and when he is returned to active ministry for a given trial period.

3. **Addictions:** Addictions refer to repeated and increased use of a substance or action that, when it is unavailable, will give rise to symptoms of distress and to the irresistible urge for the substance or action. Common addictions in priests include chemical, i.e., alcohol and drugs, sexual, and behavioral addictions. Workaholism, gambling, and overeating are common behavioral addictions. The presence of one or more

addictions significantly complicates the treatment and recovery process. These include sexual addiction—sexual activity that has become unmanageable, progressively worsens, and results in negative outcomes.

4. **Opaque Character:** Opaqueness of character refers to a projected socially acceptable persona or public self that differs from one's private persona or personal self (Sperry 1995). The purpose of this projection is to deceive and prevent others from knowing one's actual sentiments, feelings, and beliefs, or one's real agenda that is considered socially unacceptable. On the other hand, transparency of character refers to a level of openness regarding one's feelings, beliefs, and actions. With transparent character one's public self and personal self are essentially the same. In the vernacular, "what you see is what you get." Priests who are transparent can openly admit faults or mistakes and are capable of confronting sinful or unethical behavior directly rather than minimizing, avoiding, or hiding it. Opaqueness often connotes leading a double life, that is, managing an impression of integrity and propriety in public, while at the same time engaging in various activities that lack integrity or are morally reprehensible in private. For instance, an individual may appear hardworking, sober, and upright to his fellow employees, while on weekends he may be a binge drinker or be high on drugs. Similarly, a priest may be regarded as concerned and self-sacrificing in a parish assignment during the day, while at night he may cruise the streets or the Internet seeking to seduce adolescents. Often, but not always, opaque character is noted in individuals with severe personality disorders, particularly the narcissistic, antisocial, borderline, and paranoid personality disorders. Opaqueness increases with the level of severity, i.e., priests with Types IV and V inevitably lead double lives and not surprisingly show poor rehabilitation potential.

5. **Relapse and Recidivism:** Recidivism refers to a pattern of repeated relapses. Relapses are defined as slipping or reverting back to a problematic behavior, such as sexual misconduct. Relapse and recidivism are not uncommon in sexually offending priests, particularly those who have impulsive characters, untreated sexual appetites, and/or concurrent addictions (Gonsiorek 1999). Nevertheless, the best predictor of relapse and recidivism is opportunity and access. When offending priests are reassigned to the same environment or placed in similar assignments in different geographic locations, but in which they have access and opportunity to potential sexual victims, there is an extremely high probability they will offend again. Relapse and recidivism occur

even after long-term treatment that appears to be successful. Recidivism can, and often does, follow a period of one or more years of abstinence. Significant stressors and access to vulnerable individuals or potential victims are likely to trigger relapse or recidivism. Relapse and recidivism almost always indicate that a change in ministry is mandatory, either to an assignment in which there is no access to potential victims or to complete removal from active ministry.

Table 10-2 summarizes these criteria.

Some Guidelines for Utilizing the Criteria

This section provides some guidelines decision-makers may want to consider.

Guideline 1: *Assess each of the five decisional criteria in addition to the type of sexual misconduct.*

Observation: It is not uncommon for psychological and psychiatric consultants to provide a recommendation to religious leaders and superiors regarding the decision-makers' stand to retain or remove a priest from active ministry based primarily on the nature of the presentation, with the sexual predator, i.e., Type VI, believed to have the least rehabilitative potential (Gonsiorek 1999). While in and of itself the nature of the presentation has considerable value, it provides only one perspective. Experience suggests that multiple criteria can provide a fuller picture of an individual priest within a broader perspective. Such additional information should increase the probability that the decision to change a priest's status, with regard to active ministry, is rational, reasonable, and justifiable.

Guideline 2: *With a very high level of severity—as in the Type VI sexual predator—consider removing the priest from active ministry.*

Observation: While there is little doubt that the most severe form of sexual misconduct involving a classic sexual predator (Type VI) would probably warrant removal from active ministry, it should be noted that there are relatively few Type VI priests. Even though such offenders are highly publicized in the media, most religious leaders and superiors as well as lay review panels will probably only occasionally, if ever, consider such cases. More common are priests whose profiles resemble Type II, III, and IV. In such instances the other five criteria can be particularly useful in the decision process.

Guideline 3: *With moderate to high levels of severity, i.e., Type III, IV, and V, consider removal if there is at least one other criterion present.*

Table 10-2: Five Decisional Criteria

Criteria	Brief Description
Severity	refers to the grievousness of the misconduct in terms of number of victims, extent of planning, cunning, and intimidation, level of remorse, and prognosis or rehabilitation potential. The more severe Types, i.e., V and VI (Types of Clergy Sexual Misconduct) typically have poor to very poor rehabilitation potential and outcomes, while Type I tends to have much better outcomes.
Treatment Response	refers to the outcomes of formal treatment. Even though prognosis is specified in the Types, the actual treatment response is a function of the priest's motivation and efforts, as well as the superior's expectations and involvement, and the capacity to monitor high-risk priests after completion of treatment; poor motivation and involvement inevitably leads to poor rehabilitation outcomes.
Addictions	refers to repeated and increased use of a substance or action which when deprived gives rise to symptoms and irresistible urge for the substance or action; include: sexual, alcohol or drugs; or behavioral, i.e., gambling, overeating, workaholism, etc. The presence of addictions potentially complicates treatment and often compromises rehabilitation potential and outcomes.
Opaqueness of Character	refers to a projected socially acceptable persona that differs from one's actual self for the purpose of shielding one's real sentiments or agenda that is socially unacceptable. Often involves leading a double life. The greater the opaqueness the poorer the rehabilitation potential.
Relapse and Recidivism	refers to repeated relapses (relapse = reverting to a problematic behavior) even after formal treatment; recidivism can, and often does, follow a period of one or more years of abstinence. Relapse and recidivism almost always indicate limitation or removal from active ministry.

Guideline 4: *With a moderate level of severity, i.e., Type II, consider removal if there are at least two other criteria present.*

Guideline 5: *With a low level of severity, i.e., Type I, and no other criteria, there may be little, if any, indication for removal, unless the situation becomes more severe; if two or more criteria, consider removal.*

Guideline 6: *If the accusation occurred some time ago, and the level of severity was low, Type I, and there has been no subsequent accusation or legal action, consider retaining the priest in active ministry.*

Guideline 7: *If the accusation occurred some time ago, and the level of severity was moderate, Type II, and there has been no subsequent accusation or legal action, and there has been some indication of treatment and rehabilitation, consider retaining the priest in active ministry with the provision that monitoring be arranged.*

Table 10-3 summarizes these guidelines.

Table 10-3: Guidelines for Decisions about Removal or Retention

1: *Assess each of the five decisional criteria, not just type of sexual misconduct.*
2: *With a very high level of severity—as in the Type VI sexual predator—and at least one other criterion, consider removing the priest from active ministry.*
3: *With a high level of severity, i.e., Type III, IV, and V, consider removal if there is at least one other criterion present.*
4: *With a moderate level of severity, i.e., Type II, consider removal if there are at least two other criteria present.*
5: *With a low level of severity, i.e., Type I, and no other criteria, there is little, if any, indication for removal unless the situation becomes more severe; if two or more criteria, consider removal.*
6: *If the accusation occurred some time ago, and the level of severity was low, Type I, and there has been no subsequent accusation or legal action, consider retaining the priest in active ministry.*
7: *If the accusation occurred some time ago, and the level of severity was moderate, Type II, and there has been no subsequent accusation or legal action, and there has been some indication of treatment and rehabilitation, consider retaining the priest in active ministry with the provision that monitoring be arranged.*

Application of the Criteria to the Case Examples

The case of Rev. Bill Graven is consistent with Type I. His naiveté was apparent in his agreement to provide counseling when he had little training and experience in dealing with the complex transference and boundary issues that are common in such pastoral situations. Later, he would learn in the legal complaint against him that the woman had been diagnosed with borderline personality disorder, characterized by intense, unstable interpersonal relationships and boundary difficulties. Neither did the priest seem to be aware of the ethical gray areas nor the appropriate limits that are necessary to establish and maintain in such situations; nor how his loneliness and despondency following his grandfather's death would increase his vulnerability to sexual impropriety. Given that he functioned quite effectively for nearly twenty years without any other instances of sexual impropriety, had met none of the decisional criteria—low severity, no addictions, no treatment nor recidivism, and exhibited a remarkably transparent character—a strong case could be made for applying Guideline 6. In short, the recommendation would be that he *not* be removed from active ministry.

Rev. Sharff's presentation is consistent with Type V based on his charm, grandiosity, entitlement, and capacity to draw a following of loyal supporters around him. During the investigation the following pattern emerged: the priest appears to have carefully chosen his alleged victims from among those who came to him for "counseling"; all were from single-parent families, all were loners, and all had issues involving low self-esteem. When the bishop ordered him to undergo an extensive psychiatric evaluation, he objected vehemently. In time it because clear that he had no empathy or remorse for his victims and simply excused his behavior "as giving them the fatherly care they never had." No obvious addictions were diagnosed. It is noteworthy that during his inpatient and residential treatment, Sharff assumed the role of self-appointed co-therapist in his group, helping others to "get to the bottom" of their problems. Unfortunately, his own response to treatment was adjudged to be minimal given his denial of having a problem, as well as his opaqueness of character. Not surprisingly, Sharff relapsed some nine months after release from treatment even though he was reassigned to a chaplaincy at the nursing home. Unfortunately, the nursing home was only three blocks away from the high school to which he had been previously assigned, affording him indirect, but easy access to adolescent males. Regrettably, even though his post-discharge plan specified ongoing, daily monitoring of the priest, the diocese never got around to implementing the recommendation. Criminal charges were dismissed for four of the six alleged victims because the statute of limitations had run out, but court dates were set for the two other alleged victims. In this case, applying the decisional criteria—and Guideline 3—would result in a decision to remove Rev. Sharff from active ministry.

Table 10-4 illustrates this the application of the decisional criteria to both cases.

Table 10-4: Application of Criteria to the Case Examples

Criteria	Rev. Bill Graven	Rev. Andy Sharff
Severity	**Low**—brief liaison with one adult female; charges dropped; no planning or cunning; considerable guilt and remorse	**High**—ephebophilia; several adolescent victims; legal charges pending; planned and cunning; no guilt nor remorse
Treatment Response	————	**Poor**—treatment response because of denial; initially refused psychiatric evaluation
Addictions	————	————
Opaqueness of Character	————	Prominent
Relapse and Recidivism	————	**Yes**—relapsed after nine months following treatment

Decisions Regarding Fitness for Ministry

In addition to current concerns about removal of priests from active ministry, religious superiors, diocesan officials, and independent lay review committees are also faced with the difficult task of determining when a given individual is or is not "fit" for active ministry. While the criteria for removal from ministry exclusively focus on matters of serious sexual misconduct, there are many other less serious sexual concerns as well as serious nonsexual concerns that the NCCB's charter does not apply. Thus, the focus in this section of the chapter is on decisions regarding fitness for ministry. It may well be that being adjudged "unfit" for ministry will have the same outcome as the removal decision. However, while a positive removal decision should result in removal from any active ministry, a decision of unfitness could result in any number of courses of action ranging from immediate removal from active ministry to limitation being placed on a ministry to an ecclesial "hand slap" with no appreciable change in ministry status. The unfitness decision may be rather straightforward as when a criminal conviction for felony offense is rendered, e.g., embezzlement, but it could be quite complex and difficult, especially when ministry unfitness is confused with ministry impairment. What criteria should be used to determine ministry fitness and unfitness? This section describes several criteria and a few guidelines for applying these criteria.

Three Ministry Examples

The first case involves an associate pastor who was arrested for driving under the influence of alcohol. A short account of the incident appeared in the daily newspaper. A week prior to the arrest the rectory housekeeper observed what she described as slurred speech. While in an alcohol detoxification program it is determined that he was clinically depressed—secondary to the death of his younger brother—and was prescribed antidepressant treatment. No prior history of substance abuse or serious ministry problems were found. After a four-week hospitalization he is discharged.

The second case involves a lay music minister in a large urban parish with a reputation for being colorful and offbeat. While endearing for some, this dramatic flair had been upsetting for others who contended that eucharistic liturgies had turned into musical performances rather than occasions of worship. He downplayed allegations of being "touchy-feely" with married female parishioners. Complaints of being self-absorbed, demanding, indifferent to others' needs, and noncompliance with the pastor's directives and limit-setting were also noted. Nevertheless, the pastor enjoyed the type of liturgical music played and was reluctant to support the parish council's plan not to renew the minister's contract.

The third case involves a nun who is diocesan coordinator of RCIA programs. Although possessing excellent credentials, her performance had not matched her promise. She was absent or late for appointments, inconsistent in the supervision of her staff, and had failed to respond to her boss's coaching on handling staff matters. She reportedly loses her temper and cries following the least of interpersonal slights. At a recent budget meeting she raised eyebrows when she screamed out that if the bishop and chancellor really cared about her or RCIA candidates they would not cut her budget. Her personal life is reported to be chaotic, and her associates wonder if the scars on her wrists represent suicide gestures.

On first glance, it might seem that the priest with the newspaper-reported drinking problem and arrest would be unfit for ministry, while the music minister and RCIA coordinator, although troublesome, are probably fit for ministry, if not in their present jobs, at least in some other. Those who indicated that the priest was unfit probably based their determination on a criterion like public scandal. There are problems with the use of a single criterion like scandal. For instance, a priest's intoxication may not as much as raise eyebrows in one community, while it may ignite a firestorm in another. Furthermore, what constitutes scandal for a child is likely to be different from what constitutes scandal for an adult. For this reason, additional criteria can be useful in determining whether an individual is fit or not for engaging in active ministry.

Moral, Spiritual, and Psychological Ideals in Ministry

The proposed criteria reflect basic moral, spiritual, and psychological ideals deemed essential to Christian ministry. These ideals include honesty, integrity, self-surrender, and transparency of character. It is presumed that the more the minister strives after these ideals, the more likely the minister will function as a credible and effective witness of the Gospel, and vice versa. Thus, a ministry based on honesty and integrity is preferable to one based on dishonesty, misrepresentation, pretense, and lack of integrity. Furthermore, a ministry centered on the Lord and characterized by self-surrender and generosity is preferable to one that is based on self-aggrandizement and self-serving actions. Similarly, a minister who strives to be transparent and genuine in dealings with others is preferable to a minister who is gamey or opaque. There are no surprises with transparent ministers: they are who they represent themselves to be. On the other hand, there are surprises with ministers with opaque characters, as they often lead double lives. For instance, in time it comes to light that the associate pastor or music minister who has been so enthusiastic with the youth ministry is actually a sex offender.

Corresponding to these moral and spiritual ideals are certain psychological features. The more ministers strive toward these moral and spiritual ideals, the more likely they are to be helpful and collaborative, to be forgiving and conciliatory, and to be empathic and compassionate. Furthermore, they are less likely to be self-absorbed and self-serving, to demand to be the center of attention, to control and manipulate others, to seek revenge, and to be indifferent to the needs of others.

In short, individuals fit for ministry strive for the Christian ideals of transparency, integrity, honesty, self-surrender, and compassion over opaqueness of character, lack of integrity, dishonesty, and self-serving actions (Sperry 1995). Table 10-5 summarizes these themes.

Table 10-5: Moral Indicators of Fitness/Unfitness for Ministry*

Fit for Ministry	Unfit for Ministry
1. Honesty	1. Dishonesty
2. Integrity	2. Lack of Integrity
3. Self-surrender	3. Self-serving actions
4. Transparency of character	4. Opaqueness of character

* based on Sperry 1995

For the most part, the severe personality disorders, particularly the reactive or malignant narcissistic personality disorder, reflect the "unfit for ministry" indicators, and their corresponding psychological features.

Criteria for Ministry Fitness/Unfitness

The following criteria can be useful in discerning whether an individual is fit or not for engaging in active ministry. While these criteria involve observable maladaptive behavior and are psychologically based, they also reflect the basic moral and spiritual ideals of honesty, integrity, and compassion in ministry. Six criteria can be specified, with the first being the basic criterion and the others being supportive criteria:

1. A consistent pattern of opaqueness of character, lack of integrity, dishonesty, and self-serving action. Such a pattern usually characterizes a severe personality disorder, particularly the narcissistic, antisocial, borderline, or paranoid personality disorders. The presence of such psychiatric disorders as major depressive disorder, bipolar disorder (manic-depression) or panic disorder in the *absence* of one of these severe personality disorders would not necessarily indicate unfitness for ministry. On the other hand, psychiatric disorders that severely limit the individual's ability to remain in contact with reality or relate to others, such as schizophrenia, delusional disorder, dissociative disorder, severe obsessive-compulsive disorder, or a chronic, incapacitat-

ing substance-dependence disorder, might render that individual unfit for active ministry.

2. Unwillingness to participate in or unresponsiveness to coaching, spiritual direction, or other limit-setting efforts to change or ameliorate the maladaptive pattern. Poor responsivity may involve unwillingness to participate in or unresponsiveness to specific directives or other limit-setting efforts to change or ameliorate the sexual or related concern.

3. Refusal to comply with a referral for psychiatric treatment (inpatient, residential, medication evaluation, or individual or group therapy). It could also involve failure to meet treatment goals and improve sufficiently. Priests may respond in various ways ranging from a high level of agreement and responsivity, to initial agreement but little or no responsivity, to open defiance of the request or demand.

4. Criminal behavior, whether or not it results in criminal charges and conviction, severe problems with authority, i.e., continued defiance or rule-breaking, or less serious sexual improprieties, such as sexual touches, sexual harassment, or the paraphilias, such as voyeurism. Excluded is the paraphilia of pedophilia which is considered under the decisional criteria for removal from ministry.

5. The presence of one or more addictions can further complicate matters. Addictions may include substance addiction, relationship addiction, or behavioral addiction such as overeating, gambling, or workaholism.

6. Significant concern about the impact of the individual minister's behavior, or a career history marked by inconsistency or poor performance in ministerial duties impacting the spiritual and psychological well-being of those being ministered. Examples are spreading harmful rumors; physical, verbal, or emotional abusiveness; being chronically late or absent from assignments; or being the source of scandal.

Generally speaking, the first criterion plus one or more of the supporting criteria are strongly suggestive of unfitness for ministry. Two exceptions are noted: (1) if the individual does not meet all the DSM-IV-TR diagnostic criteria for a severe personality disorder (American Psychiatric Association, 2000), then three or more of the supportive criteria of unfitness should be present; and (2) a single criterion, such as admission of guilt and conviction of a felony offense such as homicide or embezzlement, is probably indicative of unfitness. On the other hand, arrest and conviction for driving under the influence of alcohol without the presence of a severe personality disorder or another of the above criteria would not necessarily qualify for unfitness. Table 10-6 summarizes these criteria.

Table 10-6: Criteria for Ministry Fitness/Unfitness**

The following criteria can be useful in discerning whether an individual is fit or not for engaging in active ministry. While these criteria involve observable maladaptive behavior and are psychologically based, they also reflect the basic moral and spiritual ideals of honesty, integrity, and compassion in ministry. Six criteria can be specified, with the first being the basic criterion and the others being supportive criteria:

1. A consistent pattern of opaqueness of character, lack of integrity, dishonesty, and self-serving action. Such a pattern usually characterizes a severe personality disorder.

2. Unwillingness to participate in or unresponsiveness to coaching, spiritual direction, or other limit-setting efforts to change or ameliorate the maladaptive pattern.

3. Refusal to comply with a referral for psychiatric treatment or failure to meet treatment goals and improve sufficiently.

4. Criminal behavior, whether or not it results in criminal charges and conviction, or severe problems with authority, such as continued defiance or rule-breaking.

5. Presence of a substance addiction, relationship addiction, or behavioral addiction such as gambling or workaholism.

6. Significant concern about the impact of the individual minister's behavior, or a career history marked by inconsistency or poor performance in ministerial duties impacting the spiritual and psychological well-being of those being ministered.

Generally speaking, the first criterion plus one or more of the supporting criteria are strongly suggestive of unfitness for ministry. Two exceptions are noted: (1) if the individual does not meet all the DSM-IV-TR diagnostic criteria for a severe personality disorder, then three or more of the supportive criteria of unfitness should be present; and (2) a single criterion, such as admission of guilt and conviction of a felony offense such as homicide or embezzlement, is usually indicative of unfitness. On the other hand, arrest and conviction for driving under the influence of alcohol without the presence of a severe personality disorder or another of the above criteria would not necessarily qualify for unfitness.

**(adapted from Sperry 2000:119)

Ministry Impairment Compared to Unfitness for Ministry

A basic psychological tenet is that personality and character are stable and relatively impervious to change. Unfortunately, this means that the prognosis for most, if not all, individuals who are determined to be unfit for ministry by the above criteria is very guarded. Unfitness must be distinguished from impairment since there is some overlap between the two.

Generally speaking, impairment involves a serious medical or psychiatric condition that greatly reduces or prevents individuals from performing most or all of their ministerial functions. On the other hand, individuals adjudged unfit to minister can often perform aspects of their ministry functions sufficiently well enough to avoid early detection. Impairments are potentially treatable and may be curable. For instance, many common psychiatric disorders such as depression, bipolar disorder, anxiety disorders, and even alcohol abuse are very amenable to psychiatric treatment and have fair to good prognoses. This contrasts with the severe personality disorders that are much less amenable to treatment and thus have poor prognoses. Personality disorders may be present in some, but not all, impaired ministers. However, severe personality disorders are almost always present in unfit ministers. Accordingly, the prognosis for those individuals adjudged unfit for ministry is very guarded or poor. Unfortunately, this effectively limits options for unfit ministers. Thus, in order to reduce chaos or unrest in a religious community, parish, or diocesan office, as well as reduce legal liability, many, if not most of these individuals are removed from active ministry. Furthermore, it is conceivable, though rare, that a minister can be both impaired and unfit for ministry.

Ministry Examples Revisited

Returning to the cases, it should now be apparent that the priest arrested for driving under the influence would not meet the criteria for ministry unfitness. Although there is evidence of Axis I disorders—major depression and alcohol abuse—there is no indication of a severe Axis II personality disorder, or refusal to comply with treatment or limit-setting, or obvious scandal—only the housekeeper had witnessed the slurred speech on a single occasion. Since no mention was made of failure to function ministerially, it is also unlikely that impairment is present. Thus, he would not be adjudged "unfit for ministry."

While it may appear that the other two cases are less serious, reviewing them in light of the proposed criteria suggests that they are much more serious. In fact, both meet criteria for ministry unfitness. The nun meets three of the six criteria. She would meet criteria for borderline personality disorder, one of the most severe and difficult to treat Axis II disorders. Additional criteria include unresponsiveness to coaching provided by her boss, and significant inconsistency in her job performance.

Similarly, the music minister meets four of the six criteria. A narcissistic personality disorder with antisocial or psychopathic features is present in the music minister. His defiance of the pastor's authority, unresponsiveness to the pastor's limit-setting, and significant concerns about the impact of his behavior on parishioners, e.g., touching the behinds of certain women, as well as empathic deficits, suggest his unfitness for this and probably any other active ministry. Since no allegation of more serious sexual misconduct, such as sexual intercourse, is noted, the so-called "zero tolerance" policy would not be applicable and presumably this individual would probably not be removed from ministry even though he would be considered "unfit for ministry." The reader may wonder: Shouldn't individuals who meet criteria for being "unfit for ministry" also be "removed from ministry"? At the present time, it appears that serious sexual impropriety is the primary concern of the episcopate as a condition for formal removal of priests from ministry, i.e., laicization.

Concluding Note

Because the wide-ranging consequences of removing a priest from active ministry are significant, this chapter offered both criteria and guidelines for assisting in making an informed and reasoned decision. Similarly, because some less serious forms of sexual impropriety and other nonsexual matters are of concern to religious leaders as well as parishioners, the chapter also provided criteria and guidelines for assessing the fitness or lack of fitness for ministry. While it seems that serious sexual misconduct is the primary and most common reason for removal from ministry, there are several other nonsexual matters that also merit removal from ministry. There are also numbers of less serious sexual improprieties and nonsexual matters that are indicative of unfitness for ministry. Presumably, both sets of criteria will be helpful for decision-makers. The challenge for the Church and its leadership is to further develop and refine operational criteria as well as guidelines for specifying reasonable sanctions for differing kinds of unfitness.

References

American Psychiatric Association. (2000). *Diagnostic and Statistical Manual of Mental Disorders, Fourth Edition-Text Revision (DSM-IV-TR)*. Washington. D.C.: American Psychiatric Association.

Gonsiorek, J. (1999). "Forensic Psychological Evaluation in Clergy Abuse." In T. Plante, ed., *Bless Me Father for I Have Sinned: Perspectives on Sexual Abuse Committed by Roman Catholic Priests*. Westport, Conn.: Praeger. 27–58.

Sperry, L. (1995). "Unfit to Minister." *Human Development* 16 (4) 35–37.

Sperry, L. (2000). Appendix. "Fitness for Ministry: Indicators and Criteria." In L. Sperry, *Ministry and Community: Recognizing, Healing and Preventing Ministry Impairment*. Collegeville: Liturgical Press. 114–21.

Chapter 11

Preventing Sexual Misconduct
in Ministry

The Chinese character for change is composed of the symbols for crisis and opportunity. When it comes to the matter of sexual misconduct in ministry, it seems incredulous that there could be any opportunity amid the anguishing crises that Church leaders face today. Yet, truly effective ministry leaders have the capacity for envisioning a better future and preventing past mistakes, in addition to the capacity for damage control and crisis management. Such effective ministry leadership is prevention-oriented rather than simply crisis-oriented. It focuses on healing and wholeness.

This chapter focuses on prevention of sexual misconduct in ministry. Prevention can be understood as a continuum involving three types of prevention. The three types are: primary, secondary, and tertiary prevention. Tertiary prevention focuses on rehabilitation, i.e., efforts to contain or slow the progression of damage from a serious impairment. Psychotherapy and other psychiatric treatments with impaired ministers are forms of tertiary prevention. Secondary prevention involves identifying or treating a problem early enough to arrest or reverse early signs of ministry impairment. Primary prevention involves efforts to avoid ministry impairment before it occurs. Healing of ministers and communities takes place across this prevention continuum.

The leaders of a religious organization play a critical role in each of these three types of prevention. But, unquestionably, the most effective religious leaders are those who focus their efforts on the primary prevention of ministry impairment (Sperry 1993).

Typically, religious leaders have dealt with sexual misconduct and other forms of ministry impairment by referring the impaired minister for psychiatric or substance-abuse treatment—tertiary prevention. Granted, the decision to initiate such a referral was necessary, it is seldom sufficient. Invariably, organizational dynamics are also involved. Therefore, policies, reward and sanction systems, and norms must be modified in order to reduce the likelihood of additional impairment—primary prevention. It may require a change in personnel—secondary prevention—such as removing a popular or highly visible minister from active service because he is no longer morally, spiritually, or psychologically fit for ministry. Needless to say, prevention efforts are unlikely to be successful unless the leadership of an organization fully supports and leads the change effort. Whatever the case, discernment, decisiveness, and courageousness are essential features of effective leadership that is visionary. In other words, prevention of ministry impairment requires visionary leadership.

This chapter will briefly define and delineate the concept of visionary leadership in ministry, along with its requisite skills and components. It will describe and illustrate visionary leadership with sexual misconduct involving ministry personnel.

Visionary Leadership in Ministry

Today, the business and management literature is inundated with articles, chapters, and books on leadership, particularly visionary leadership. Visionary leadership has been described as the action of the leader who takes charge, makes things happen, dreams and then translates them into reality. The roles of direction-setting, change agent, coach, and spokesperson define the job of the visionary leader (Nanus 1992). Burt Nanus, director of the Leadership Institute at the University of Southern California, provides a formula for successful visionary leadership: *successful visionary leadership = shared purpose (+) vision (+) communication (+) strategic thinking (+) appropriate organizational changes (+) empowered personnel.*

So what does visionary leadership have to do with preventing sexual misconduct and impairment in ministry? Everything!

Types of Responses to the Sexual Misconduct Crisis

There are at least four different types of responses that episcopal authorities can make to this crisis. The first type of response basically involves denial: refusal to investigate, minimizing, ignoring, or blaming the victim. The second type of response involves various reactive initiatives, such as setting up review commissions, establishing policy statements, insuring treatment is offered the victims, or advocating for the laicization of the perpetrators. The third type involves proactive and/or preventive initiatives. The guidelines for seminary training and celibacy and human sexual development in the NCCB's document *The Program of Priestly Formation* (1982) and Jesuit physician James Gill's (1993) establishment of the Christian Institute for the Study of Human Sexuality are examples of preventive and proactive initiatives. A fourth type of response involves initiatives based on strategic planning and principles.

Strategic planning is a process in which the leaders of an organization or institution envision its future and develop the necessary goals and procedures for achieving that future. Strategically managed organizations have clearly articulated and appropriated vision or mission statements that galvanize members' commitment and guide their efforts in accomplishing the organization's goals. By definition, strategically emerged organizations are visionary and proactive rather than crisis-oriented and reactive.

Organizations vary in the degree to which they are strategically managed and led. In *Archbishop,* a detailed analysis of the Catholic Church's power structure, Reese (1989) states that episcopal governance is "primarily reactive and not proactive" and typically engages in crisis management. He observes that while some archdioceses have developed mission statements and pastoral plans, few do strategic planning, and most episcopal decision-making is incremental (short-term, crisis-oriented) rather than comprehensive (long-term and future-oriented). Finally, Reese notes that "where planning is taking place, it is usually in response to a perceived crisis such as the decline in the number of priests."

What is the vision and mission of the American Catholic Church? Do most of its members know and understand this mission statement? Are their thoughts, decisions, and behaviors guided by this mission? The answers are likely: probably not, no, and no. Herein, I believe, is the core problem. As the psalmist says: "Without a vision the people perish."

Some would agree that, when society is relatively stable and un-changing, the mission of primary social institutions does not have to be explicitly stated because everyone knows what the Church is about, what the family should be and what community government stands for. However, in times of rapid change and increased complexity and instability, institutional missions change and need to be clearly articulated. Reese argues that, since Vatican II, bishops have had to face a more complex and constantly changing environment, and lacking consensus on goals and lacking certainty on effectiveness, bishops have found themselves in the worst possible position to make what have been traditionally considered "rational" decisions.

Reese contends that one reason episcopal leaders favor incremental planning over comprehensive and strategic planning is their lack of sophistication in the social sciences. I contend that political realities and economic necessity could reverse this view. Probably more than anytime in the recent past, the need for a proactive leader using visionary leadership skills has never been more evident.

But is visionary leadership compatible with Christian organizations? It could be argued that Jesus exemplifies the best of visionary leadership. The ministry of Paul clearly reflects a visionary leadership. The same could be said of many founders of religious orders, as well as the first bishop of the United States, John Carroll. The recent biography of Ignatius of Loyola implies that the founder of the Society of Jesus was a master of visionary leadership (Meissner 1992).

Visionary Leadership and Preventing Sexual Misconduct

So how would visionary leadership deal with the sexual misconduct crisis? Basically, it would not have permitted this situation to escalate into its present crisis proportions. Rather, visionary leadership would prevent crises from occurring.

Let's look at how visionary leadership could be applied to ministry to prevent further and future impairment based on Nanus' formula for successful visionary leadership. Recall that he describes visionary leadership as the practice of involving and orchestrating shared purpose and vision, communication, strategic thinking, appropriate organizational changes, and empowered personnel.

Vision and Shared Purpose. The first priority would be to clearly articulate the overall vision and mission of the American Catholic Church and the specific roles of clergy, religious, and other laity in achieving this mission. A forum consisting of representative stake-holders in the Church, i.e., hierarchy, priests, religious, and other lay-people, would be involved in envisioning and discussing this shared purpose. The importance of psychosexual development and the mean-ing of celibacy and chastity in ministry personnel would be among the topics to be articulated.

Communication. This vision and shared purpose would need to be communicated, that is, shared and discussed at the grassroots level to the point where the vision is understood and accepted. Visionary leaders attempt to galvanize commitment of followers to the vision and shared purpose.

Strategic Thinking. Strategic thinking is a necessary process in implementing a shared vision and purpose. Strategic thinking reduces vague and muddled thinking and wishes. When episcopal leaders and ministry personnel practice strategic thinking, they would likely con-sider how Jesus might act and respond in a given situation. When the matter of preventing sexual misconduct is considered, seminary and formation personnel would strategically discuss ways of (1) modify-ing a religious organization's structures and culture to prevent sexual misconduct, as well as (2) implementing guidelines on training candi-dates about celibacy, i.e., NCCB's The Program of Priestly Formation, as well as the NCCB's charter.

Appropriate Organizational Change. Next the Church's organi-zation at its various levels would be examined for the purpose of re-configuring structures, cultures, and leadership style to support and insure that the mission would be accomplished (Sperry 1990). Obvi-ously, this would be a major undertaking and would start at points of greater need. Regarding sexual misconduct, several commentators note that the Church's culture of secrecy probably disposes and per-petuates sexual misconduct. Cozzens (2002) indicates that the cul-ture of secrecy and denial within the Church is destructive to sexual responsibility by shielding sexual impropriety and thereby unwittingly reinforcing it. This culture of secrecy, while on the one hand providing confidentiality and "not giving scandal," has the effect of institution-ally insulating the system in such a way that perpetuates the very problem it was designed to eradicate. Visionary leadership would modify this institutional culture accordingly and quickly. Further-more, the crisis management style of episcopal leadership and its em-phasis on short-term incremental planning would be replaced with long-range strategic planning.

Empowered Ministry Personnel. Finally, when "people buy into the vision, they possess the authority, that is, they are empowered to take actions that advance the vision, knowing that such actions will be highly valued by all those who share the dream" (Nanus 1992). Empowerment is frequently discussed among ministry personnel but less often demonstrated, probably because episcopal leaders are not convinced of its values or are afraid of its impact. Nevertheless, visionary leaders empower individuals and these individuals then respond with effective, responsible behavior. Regarding sexual misconduct: when Catholic ministers and the people they work with are empowered to form their consciences and are expected to act respectfully and responsibly, sexual exploitation would be reduced or eliminated.

Does application of the visionary leadership formula and principles seem unrealistic and unlikely to be achieved in the American Church at this time? If it was possible, how long would it take? In organizations, including religious organizations, the usual time span for transitioning from a traditional mode of operation to a visionary mode of operations is 2.5–5 years, even among large multinational corporations. It is not unreasonable to think that it would take at least that amount of time, or more, for a given diocese or province to change.

Strategies for Prevention of Sexual Misconduct

Abusive ministers can be incredibly hurtful and demoralizing to those who work with them and ministries invariably suffer also. There is a tendency for religious leaders to assume that psychotherapy or a psychiatric referral is the answer to the problem of abusive behavior. Unfortunately, while such referral may sometimes help, the more basic concern is preventing abusiveness within the diocese, religious community, parish, or other ministry setting. Such preventive strategies include the abusive minister, the religious organization's culture, and the specific ministry situation.

Deal Directly with Abusive Ministers

The first strategy involves dealing directly with the abusive minister. Since treatment is an aspect of tertiary prevention, it is essential that these ministry personnel are expected to participate and make changes in the treatment process. Previously, chapter 5 described the abusive personalities as deeply wounded because of their experience of early life abuse, shame, and insecure attachment. It is unrealistic to expect that personal effort, spiritual direction, medication to control aggressivity, or involvement in a general form of psychotherapy will easily modify and heal these deep wounds. The research of Dutton (1998) and others (Landolt and Dutton 1997) suggests that most individual and group psychotherapy is ineffective with abusive personalities, particularly the antisocial personality or "psychopathic type" as Dutton calls them. On the other hand, a referral to a psychotherapist with a proven track record in treating borderline personality disorders may reduce abusive behavior, the "cyclical type," while therapy with the "overcontrolled type" has a better prognosis (Dutton 1998). Whether therapy is indicated or not, there is no question that alcohol and other drugs tend to exacerbate abusiveness. Accordingly, a key consideration is to secure the commitment of the abusive minister to become substance-free, which may require detoxification and substance-abuse counseling or a support group.

Deal with Organizational Factors

Every religious congregation and diocese has a unique corporate culture, i.e., the constellation of beliefs, assumptions, stories, procedures, and customs that characterize an organization. Corporate cultures can be healthy or unhealthy, abuse-prone, or abuse-free. Religious institutions and clerical culture have been described as control- and power-oriented. It should not be too surprising, then, that abusive behavior is not uncommon in religious organizations. Furthermore, religious organizations that have abuse-prone cultures are more likely to attract, reinforce, and retain abusive individuals than are religious organizations with more abuse-free cultures (Sperry 2000). There are two strategies of effectively changing a religious organization's culture to be less abuse-prone: (1) establish admission and screening policies to exclude abuse-prone candidates; and (2) modify the organization's strategy and structure to foster an abuse-free environment.

Select Healthy Candidates

Formation personnel and administrators of dioceses and other religious organizations have several responsibilities regarding ministerial sexual abuse. While chapter 8 focuses in detail on candidate selection, this section reiterates a few points and adds a couple of others.

The first responsibility involves a policy on the suitability of candidates. Perhaps the most basic policy question is: Will we knowingly accept and encourage abusive individuals to enter professional ministries? If the answer is no, that committee will then make the requisite decisions to structure its screening and assessment process to rule out candidates with psychological assessment protocols sensitized to abusive personality and histories indicative of habitual abusive behavior. As a general rule, candidates who meet criteria for severe personality disorders are a mismatch for active ministries given that abusive behavior is characteristic of most severe and even moderate personality pathology, particularly borderline personality disorder and antisocial personality disorder, also known as the psychopathic personality.

The second is a careful screening of candidates. Today, screening of potential ministers is becoming more sensitized to "risk management" issues such as concurrent psychiatric disorders, low impulse control, and medical and legal contraindications for public ministry. Traditionally, standardized psychological testing has been useful, but it cannot be the sole or main screening strategy. Clever individuals with severe personality disorders, particularly narcissistic and psychopathic personalities, can and have "passed" the scrutiny of the Minnesota Multiphasic Personality Inventory (MMPI-2), the Millon Clinical Multiaxial Inventory (MCMI-III), and other personality tests. It should be noted that many ministers who have been accused of pedophilia were "tested" before entering the seminary or novitiate.

Effective screening requires careful, in-depth interviewing by seasoned, specially trained clinicians who follow an interview protocol. This protocol should include a structured interview of the candidate's personality structure, family and developmental history, as well as social history (school, work, and military experience). Since a personality disorder is a lifelong maladaptive pattern, clues of its presence will emerge upon careful investigation. Essential background information on the applicant includes a detailed formal application form that inquires about criminal charges and convictions, marital status, psychiatric history, and a year-by-year accounting of time since high school. This should be supplemented with specific queries about the applicant's theological views, spiritual practices, and sexual attitudes and behaviors.

A set of interviews with the applicant should expand and clarify the applicant's written responses to these, including questions to ascertain the applicant's capacities and maturity to function as a minister. At least one of these interviews should seek to assess the applicant's level of emotional, spiritual, and sexual maturity. The interviewer will have to be sufficiently skilled to formulate a profile of the applicant's boundaries and boundary issues, power needs, and experience of and capacity for intimacy.

Routine background checking should be mandatory. This should include a checking for a criminal record, a query of the listed academic institutions, novitiates, or seminaries attended, as well as jobs held to verify the accuracy of information on the application. At least five letters of recommendation should be required followed up by phone inquiries of at least three of the recommenders. Presumably, such a protocol will screen out actual and at-risk applicants.

Modify Culture, Structure, and Strategy

After determining that its culture is abuse-prone, a religious organization can focus change efforts on its strategy and structure. First, its basic strategy (i.e., its vision and mission statement) and its structures (i.e., communication and reporting patterns, policies and procedures—including screening and admission policy, and its system of rewards and sanctions) are reviewed to determine how they may engender, support, and reinforce abuse-proneness (Sperry 2000). Structures that reduce and negatively sanction abusive behavior can then be instituted. Limit-setting is one such structure and is essential in containing abusive behavior in religious organizations. Since abusive personalities have a tendency to disregard rules and social conventions and breach boundaries, the religious organization must consistently expect that rules will be followed and then set limits that are clear, realistic, consistent, and enforceable. The organization must then promptly enforce these provisions. For example, if an abusive minister has been known to emotionally, verbally, or physically assault parishioners or staff, a firm limit to reestablish basic respect is needed. The decision to review the organization's policies and practices about rewards and sanctions may show that the organization unwittingly reinforces abusive behavior by fostering and rewarding competition (i.e., academic, social, sports awards, and honors), making invidious comparisons, or being inconsistent in sanctioning abusive behavior.

Evaluate Ministry Assignments and Reassignments

There are at least two main considerations regarding this preventive measure. The first involves the ministry assignment of the abusive minister while the second involves an appraisal or monitoring of the abusive minister in that assignment. Decisions about the abusive minister's current assignment need to be carefully evaluated. Whether the individual remains in the current assignment or is changed should be a function of the type and severity of abusiveness as well as the needs of other ministry personnel and those being ministered to at that site. In some instances the abusiveness is primarily directed toward one or two individuals, while in other instances, several people are the recipients of the abuse. Sometimes, when the potential for scandal is very high or morale is very low or the situation has reached an impasse, it may be necessary to reassign the abusive individual to an nonactive ministry position or status. When, however, structural changes can be put into place and/or the prognosis of psychotherapeutic intervention is fair to good, it may be possible to maintain the assignment.

An important structural component that can positively influence abusive behavior is a performance-appraisal system (Sperry 2000). It can be a quarterly or semiannual performance appraisal or a monitoring system (i.e., some dioceses mandate weekly or monthly monitoring of troublesome ministers). Whatever form it takes, some appraisal system or method can be implemented with abusive ministers and may allow that individual to remain in a particular assignment. The appraisal can focus on reducing abusive behavior with specific performance goals set and assessed. Such assessment allows for any corrective actions based on formal, documented criteria.

Formulate and Implement Prevention-Oriented Policies

Dioceses as well as religious congregations and institutions must develop realistic written policies about appropriate and inappropriate sexual behavior (Sperry 1993; 1995). The policy should include provisions about screening applicants for various ministries and specific policies and guidelines about a minister's involvement with parishioners, including informal and formal counseling. This policy statement must articulate the importance of clear boundaries and the consequences for boundary violations. It must specify the basis for reporting, internal investigation, due process, monitoring impaired ministers, cooperating with police investigations, treatment of complainants and victims, and consequences for violation of the policy, such as professional treatment, termination/removal from a ministry position, and so on. Needless to say, unless such policies are enacted and consistently upheld, ministry personnel will quickly realize that the policy has no teeth or that loopholes exist. Predictably, personality-disordered ministers will avail themselves of these shortcomings.

A number of dioceses and religious congregations have already established this type of policy statement hoping to delimit their legal and financial liabilities. This is an important first step. The next step is to articulate a policy about educating all ministry personnel about human sexuality in relationship to developmental psychology and religious and spiritual development. This type of policy is proactive and prevention-oriented. It should specify how formation personnel are trained, as well as how they will insure that all other ministry personnel are likewise trained.

Expect That Misconduct Will Be Reported

The days of benignly looking beyond and ignoring a fellow minister's sexual abusing behavior hopefully are over. It is unlikely that dioceses and religious congregations will ever again presumptively deny charges of sexual misconduct or stonewall investigations. Media coverage in the past few years has made it painfully clear that civil courts have and will continue to hold dioceses and religious congregations liable for the actions of their ministers. A development that has had relatively little media coverage so far involves recently enacted "vicarious liability and negligence" laws. These laws are directed at liability against individuals rather than institutions or organizations. Essentially, under these laws a professional colleague can be held liable for the sexual misconduct of another colleague. If a professional colleague knew about or could have prevented the sexual misconduct, that colleague can also be held liable. While these laws have so far been directed at physicians' groups, it won't be long before they are directed at colleagues on parish teams and councils, provincial teams, and diocesan staffs.

Implement Post-Treatment Monitoring

After it has been determined that a sexual boundary violation has occurred, and the minister is made to undergo a rehabilitation process, a formal monitoring mechanism is usually required to maintain the rehabilitation gains and prevent relapse. This might precede or follow a civil or criminal trial. Central to this monitoring is a written agreement of objectives for the rehabilitation process and restrictions on the minister's professional and personal activities, including limitations or prohibitions on contacts with certain individuals. Only those ministry colleagues and superiors who have a need to know are privy to the written agreement. A mature, trustworthy minister is assigned the role of monitor and regularly meets with the minister in question on a daily or weekly basis initially, and then biweekly or monthly later, to review the written agreement. The monitor also contacts designated ministry colleagues to ascertain the extent to which the provisions of the agreement are being kept.

Concluding Note

Preventing ministry impairment requires the support and active involvement of religious leaders in all three types of prevention but particularly primary prevention. Truly effective leadership is not afraid to consider that, not only are impaired ministers in their organization, but their very organization may be impaired and impairing some of its members by its policies, culture, and norms. Seven individual and organizational strategies for preventing sexual misconduct and other forms of ministry impairment were detailed.

Ministry leadership has a basic choice that must be confronted. They can continue in a crisis management mode or they can choose to act with visionary leadership and implement the various suggested preventive measures. However, no single policy change or programmatic implementation—no matter how proactive—can in and of itself change individual behavior in an organization that unwittingly fosters entitlement and abusiveness. Perhaps another way of saying this is that abuse-prone religious organizations significantly influence the sexual behaviors of their ministers. To truly change or prevent sexual misconduct and other forms of impairment requires that both individual and religious organization change.

References

Cozzens, D. (2002). *Sacred Silence: Denial and the Crisis in the Church*. Collegeville: Liturgical Press.

Dutton, D. (1998). *The Abusive Personality*. New York: Guilford.

Gill, J. (1993). "Better Formation for Celibacy Needed." *Human Development* 14 (1) 3–4.

Landolt, M., and D. Dutton. (1997). "Power and Personality: An Analysis of Gay Intimate Male Abuse." *Sex Roles* 37 (5/6) 335–59.

Meissner, W. (1992). *Ignatius of Loyola: The Psychology of a Saint*. New Haven: Yale University Press.

Nanus, B. (1992). *Visionary Leadership*. San Francisco: Jossey-Bass.

National Conference of Catholic Bishops (1982). *The Program of Priestly Formation*. 3rd ed. Washington, D.C.: U.S. Catholic Conference.

Reese, T. (1989). *Archbishop: Inside the Power Structure of the American Catholic Church*. San Francisco: Harper and Row.

Sperry, L. (1990). "Blind Leadership in Stumbling Organizations." *Human Development* 11 (4) 24–29.

Sperry, L. (1993). "Preventing Impairment in Ministers." *Human Development* 14 (24) 7–10.

Sperry, L. (2000). "The Abusive Personality in Ministry." *Human Development* 21 (3) 32–36.

Index